CATHEDRALS OF EUROPE

CATHEDRALS
of EUROPE

Text by Josef Grünenfelder

Photographs by Michael Wolgensinger

Translated by David Lawrence Grambs

THOMAS Y. CROWELL COMPANY
Established 1834   New York

Designed by Abigail Moseley

PRINTED IN BELGIUM 🆈
by OFFSET VAN DEN BOSSCHE 🆅🅱

Library of Congress Cataloging in Publication Data

Grünenfelder, Josef.
    Cathedrals of Europe.

    1. Cathedrals.   I. Wolgensinger, Michael.
II. Title.
NA4830.G78   726′.6′094   76–8897
ISBN 0-690-01172-5

10 9 8 7 6 5 4 3 2 1

CONTENTS

CATHEDRALS OF EUROPE

INTRODUCTION

A cathedral, by definition, is the church of a bishop. It gets its name from the prelate's official seat, or *cathedra*, which is situated in the church and which symbolizes the role of the bishop as judge and teacher. Originally set up in the apse, the cathedra derives from the *faldistorium*, the chair of a Roman judge. The bishop's throne now has its place on the north side of the choir, or to the right as one looks out from the altar, and is distinguished by its baldachin (canopy) and steps.

The bishop's duties as teacher and arbiter in matters of faith come to him as successor to the apostles, and he himself requires consecration by another bishop, who likewise must be ordained to assure that the "apostolic succession" is preserved. Thus the bishop is not a high ecclesiastical "official"; rather, he derives his legitimacy from his place in the ordinational sequence that began with the twelve trusted disciples of Christ.

The bishop is assigned a district, known as a diocese or bishopric. The dioceses in turn make up a church province headed by an archbishop who is not merely consecrated the way the ordinary bishop is but is his superior. The division into dioceses represented the first comprehensive pan-European organization of the church after the fall of the Roman Empire.

The bishop is supported in his duties by a college of priests, the cathedral chapter, which serves and maintains the cathedral and is the constant in the relatively rapid turnover of episcopal office-holders. It was thanks to this service order that the cathedral edifice, despite decades and often century-long periods of construction, could be finished—usually with an astonishing degree of unity. While the cathedral chapters on the Continent were and are for the most part made up of secular priests, the English church was far more monastically oriented.

Like every human institution, the cathedral is subject to the vicissitudes of time. New dioceses are established, old ones are combined or given up—one need only think of the church provinces of Asia Minor in late antiquity—and new episcopal sees are founded, replaced, or lost. In the course of history churches were elevated

1

to cathedrals, others lost this higher rank to serve once again as parish churches; still others, perhaps, went over to other denominations, were profaned, or completely disappeared.

With this in mind, one may perhaps appreciate why this book describes not only cathedrals per se but former or one-time episcopal churches, such as Constance or Lausanne, and edifices that became cathedrals only after they were built, such as Venice and St. Gall. The fact that St. Peter's in Rome is represented here even though it is not a bishop's church in the true sense—Rome's official cathedral is St. John in the Lateran—needs no apology. It is, after all, the ceremonial basilica of the preeminent bishop in Christendom and the burial church of the apostle Peter; not to mention that in its apse Bernini built the magnificent "Cathedra Petri."

It is in the cathedral, the chief church of the diocese, that the bishop attends to his official business, and it is in the same building that he is buried. Being the core of the diocese, it is no wonder that it is also the center of Christian art. In the Gothic cathedrals of France, it represents nothing less than a formal embodiment of the spirit of medieval Western civilization. We instinctively associate the word "cathedral" with the image of the Gothic edifice, which the master of Chartres first made a reality. There is no question that the Gothic thirteenth and fourteenth centuries were the period of the greatest cathedral building, yet they represent but a fraction of church history. Other periods also built and regional styles flourished.

To choose a sampling of scarcely two dozen from an almost unimaginable variety of European cathedrals poses a virtual agony of selection, and deciding which among those of com-

parable excellence should be given priority and coverage was difficult indeed. There are many illustrious church buildings that do not appear in this book. On the other hand, in these pages the reader will perhaps discover new and worthy cathedrals and possibly go on to explore them for himself.

As we consider these works, it is wise to realize that our perspective is not the same as that of earlier times. Our role is one of observer and enjoyer, and when a tourist is asked his opinion of a church building he will generally respond subjectively, emotionally; to 'him it will be beautiful or ugly, plain or ornate, warm or cold.

The Middle Ages had another way of looking at things. Theological-rationalistic criteria were standard, and the very number of buttresses and portals was regarded as symbolic. The proportions had to have distinct arithmetic-musical relationships. For the physical structure was the Heavenly City, built on the support of the twelve apostles with Christ as the cornerstone. In its cross-shaped form, it signified the Savior's mystical body, the nave representing the community of believers. The light, wondrously refracted and transformed through the stained-glass windows, symbolized the light of God, ever changing as it passed through the images of events in the life of Christ and the saints.

With the Renaissance, Western civilization rediscovered the idealized beauty that typified the art of antiquity. The baroque transformed it again, particularly in architecture. Instead of a rational theology translated into architectural order, baroque cathedral art created the immediate dramatic illusion of the very entrance to heaven; the open vaults revealed the sanctified spaces. The multilayered allegory, sophisticated symbolism, personal-historical references, and subtle artistic allusions combine in the interrelationship of architecture, sculpture, plastic decoration, and painting. It is as if baroque man had a form of polyphony roiling in his mind, not only in terms of music but all the arts and in theology itself.

This resounds with special force today if one is fortunate enough to experience a high pontifical mass with music, incense, and splendid clerical raiment in a baroque church. It is as if the saints themselves, in their exultation, had descended from the kingdom of clouds, to which the more mundane clouds of incense rise. In this celestial drama, the believer can only stand in devout wonder, his responsiveness depending upon a certain sense of individual and sensuous surrender. The experience of this holy drama ideally should awaken yearnings to see, for once, the incomparably sublime reality beyond this world.

Cathedrals, like the great abbey or pilgrimage churches, have numerous more pragmatic functions. Besides the high altar, where official services such as chapter masses and high masses are held, there are various other altars which serve for the different cathedral offices, for the safekeeping of the ciborium containing the consecrated Host, or—as in the cathedral at Chur, Switzerland—as a "sacramental house," or tabernacle, from pre-Reformation times. If the cathedral serves also as a parish church, there will be a special altar for popular services; in Seville the cathedral has its own separate annex for local ceremonies. And, too, there are the chapels and sanctuaries or shrines—sometimes a part of the central nave, sometimes attached to it—which guilds, brotherhoods, and prominent families underwrote and furnished with religious appointments.

The basic shape of the Spanish cathedrals, their manifold structures often evolved over the course of centuries, is difficult to acertain from outside. In England, on the other hand, the surrounding verdant close makes the form easy to discern, and the crystalline definition of the French cathedral scarcely allows any element to detract from the carefully articulated whole. In Italy it is common to find baptisteries as independent buildings of appreciable dimensions (St. John in the Lateran, Ravenna, Florence, Pisa).

Naturally the large colleges of priests and their special ceremonial garments and apparatuses require spacious sacristies where the vestments can be stored and celebratory entrances and processions prepared. Besides the communion chalices, the clerical accouterments include monstrances, censers, reliquaries, croziers, vessels for the ceremonial washing of hands, mitres, pectoral crosses, rings, shoes, and gloves. In the cabinets hang pontifical vestments for the solemn high masses requiring many clergy and chasubles for the celebrant prelates, at least two dalmatics for deacon and subdeacon, who minister and do the readings, and pluvials or copes, stoles, and shoulder or benediction vestments. Not uncommonly the cupboards also contain extra mitres and coverings for priedieux and chalices. To accord with the changing liturgical days and seasons, differently colored hangings are required for the chancel: white (for high feast days), red (for Whitsuntide, or Pentecost, and All Saints), green (for the Sundays following Epiphany and Pentecost), violet (for penitential seasons), and black (for Good Friday and requiem masses). More seldom, the liturgical colors are blue (for the Feast of the Virgin) or pink (for the "Gaudete" in Advent and "Laetere" in Lent).

3

Let us return to the interior of the church. On both sides of te choir stand the stalls for the canons who celebrate the divine offices in antiphonal song. The word "install" (*installare*) derives from the canon in his stall or choir seat; we use the word today with far more secular denotations, although one still speaks of a priest's "installation." It is not unusual for there to be a special organ or two in this part of the church for musical accompaniment. The connection of the choir benches to the organ console took wondrous forms in the south German churches (St. Gall, Ottobeuren, Weingarten).

Actually the organ was not always the principal church musical instrument. It first made its way into churches in the Middle Ages, when great processions became common, and was literally hung on the wall as a "swallow's nest." With the ever-growing size of the instrument, hanging was no longer practical and the organ was relocated in the west gallery or loft above the entrance where it is usually found today. Among the oldest, still-functional organs are those in the Valeria Church at Sitten (Sion), Freiberg-im-Breisgau, Chartres, and Strassburg.

Now that we know a little of the bishop's church, we may marvel that the Middle Ages, with such limited construction techniques, managed to bring to completion these magnificent works. There was a supremely well developed building organization behind it all.

Usually the Gothic cathedral was the special province of the chapter, even when the initiative to build it came from the bishop. From among the various canons a construction manager was chosen who was to oversee the church construction—and, above all, its financial aspects. A building corporation or lodge was established under the direction of a proven architect. He was not an academically trained architect having trained as a stonemason, as had his subordinates. He was promoted to construction chief on the basis of talent, experience, and accomplishments. He completed the plan of the church and its details on a bed of plaster or a plank of wood, using either the square or the equilateral triangle as his basic form. The draft was kept under lock and key lest an unauthorized person pirate it. The jobs of the building laborers were not strongly delineated, except for the obvious division between the masons (stone) and the carpenters (wood). Tasks were determined according to the workers' abilities and levels of training. The completed, chiseled stones were carried to their place or hoisted to heights with cranes. Some of the medieval engineering devices are preserved, notably one at the cathedral in Constance, Switzerland. For centuries the wheel-crane at the uncompleted south tower was the distinctive feature of the Cologne cathedral. The construction lodges were generally independent and were not affiliated with the city guilds, having their own jurisdiction and their own by-laws and rules. Their members did not have to live in the city, and many masters and journeymen traveled from one lodge to another. The same was true of artists, who could move freely between countries.

In the baroque period the building organizations functioned in a similar way. But instead of a constant, standing lodge, lasting for decades if not centuries—on Gothic cathedrals stones continually had to be replaced and repairs constantly made—many ad-hoc construction troops were brought along by the appointed architect. So it was that small builders of the Bregenz forest were drawn, from spring to fall, to the great building sites of abbeys in southern Germany. The building went along quickly since it was usually no longer necessary to have carefully cut stones or to pile them in layers. Mortared quarry-stone wallwork progressed rapidly, although the architectural product was often less durable.

In the Middle Ages and the baroque period there was no concept of "purity of material" on which such great store is placed in our century. There was no hestitation about covering architectural elements and sculptures with plaster or applying color—typically red—to parts of the design. Figures of saints were warmly polychromed, sometimes naturalistically, sometimes in a distinctly stylized way. Nor did the outer structure escape color. Red, blue, and ocher were highly favored and sometimes were run in stripes around the ribs of vaults.

Moreover, in visualizing the churches as they were during the Middle Ages, we must remove the chairs we are accustomed to seeing in their naves yet remember that the buildings were filled with much more liturgical furniture than today. The restorations of the nineteenth and twentieth centuries stripped many interiors in the belief that the architectural work of art was being serviced. But by banishing the original furnishings, precious pages of architectural history were lost.

Certainly these restorations also had their merits, for without their earnestness many a cathedral would have not survived. Let us hope that our own times will be more cautious, as the works of the past are inevitably becoming ever rarer. What are perhaps most endangered today are not the cathedrals but the more modest churches and chapels of Europe—the very parishes or conventual churches which, in history, became cathedrals.

CHARTRES

The Cathedral of Notre Dame

There are three reasons for the fame of Chartres: it has been a favorite of pilgrims, is the cradle of French Gothic architecture, and has sublime stained-glass windows.

Pilgrimages were on the rise in the late ninth century after Charles the Bald sent the veil of the Virgin Mary, acquired by Charlemagne in Byzantium, to the church at Chartres. Even today the piece of cloth is among the treasures of the cathedral, and scientific examinations have shown that it is in fact a Palestinian fabric of the first century. Chartres had won the favor of the royal house and was the place to which the creator of the first Gothic choir, the Abbot Suger of Saint-Denis, called an assembly of nobles to propose a crusade. In folk culture Chartres was considered one of the "royal" cities, and in its bishop's church there were divine offices and gatherings in the presence of kings arrayed in the trappings of their power.

Chartres enjoyed its heyday in the twelfth century, when its cathedral school attained worldwide renown and when it had such eminent minds among its teachers as Thierry of Chartres and John of Salisbury. Bishop Fulbert, the builder of the Romanesque cathedral, was an inspired instructor, known to his pupils as Socrates. Thierry pursued theological mysteries by way of geometrical constructions and found the analogue of the three-personed Trinity in the equilateral triangle and the interrelation of Father and Son in the square: since God the Father was the highest Oneness and the Son the Oneness Witnessed by that Oneness, so the square was essentially the multiplication of an entity by itself. These speculations, which seem rather strange to us today, nonetheless give us some keys to the understanding of Gothic architecture. A cathedral could be defined formally, through geometry, as a palpably theological building.

The basic conception of the church as a microcosm of heaven is nowhere so direct and striking as in the ever-changing light of Gothic stained-glass windows. At Chartres they have been preserved in their entirety and are of peerless artistic quality, as shown by the rose window of the north transept.

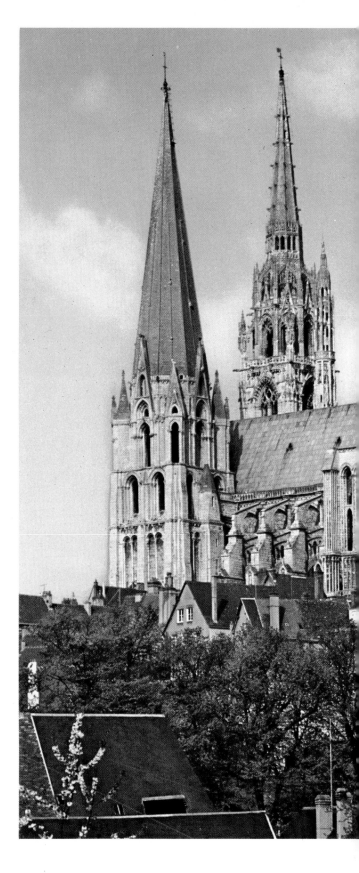

From far away the spires of Chartres can be seen rising above the city. Tower adjuncts to the transept and the choir are clearly visible on the skyline and help to make the cathedral seem a "City of God" in the most literal sense.

The sculptures in the royal portal combine human figures and columns in a distinctively pure stylization.

Is it, then, only an accident that Chartres should be called the archetype of the Gothic edifice? Or that the word "cathedral" does not call up an image of an early Christian, Romanesque, or baroque church but rather a picture of a great Gothic church with double tower, flying buttresses, and soaring linear dimensions?

The elements of the Gothic style—the pointed arch, the ribbed vault, the clustered pier, and arcades—already existed by 1194, when the eleventh-century church in Chartres burned to the ground. But what the architect—his name unknown—of the new Gothic church accomplished in less than thirty years was the creation of a unified, consistent architectural system. He dispensed with the usual gallery or choir loft and separated the arcades and central nave windows by the narrow passageway of the triforium. A crossribbed vault spanned every bay of the clerestory so that the alternation of strong and weak supports could be given up. The "cantoned" pier—the central column decorated on each side with an engaged column—was uniformly employed. The nave was tripartite, the choir five-aisled with a richly windowed garland of radial chapels. The exterior became angular and crystalline. In place of an amorphous bay arrangement a logical system of supportive members evolved, with openings which, in later development, consisted almost exclusively of colored glass.

At Chartres, to be sure, tracery was still in its beginnings. The walls were pierced with openings yet remained recognizable as whole surfaces. Later they condensed to a sinewy, stone armature interwoven with ornamentation. Everywhere one looks in this church he sees intimations of the future. And yet it is already a complete work of art. There is a spirit, a logic, that presides and overcomes all inconsistencies.

This great achievement did not arise without certain determining limitations. The reconstruction of the burned cathedral proceeded at a breathtaking pace, but the builders had to respect the basic Fulbert church structure and incorporate the west end with both towers and front into the new design. Building proceeded from west to east, to judge from the way Romanesque elements give way to Gothic, as in the buttressing. In the nave the flying buttresses are still linked with one another through small, radially placed, compact pillars beneath rounded arches, but in the choir they have become disk-shaped and lightened by ogival openings.

Nine towers should actually have risen about the structure—four on each flank with a central (crossing) tower. It may have been the Gothic tendency to shun the voluminous for the geometrical that prevented their ever being higher than the roof cornices. Only the older west towers remain. The northern one received its elegant spire in the Late Gothic period, appropriately signifying the end of the Gothic idiom at the very place of its origin. The term "Gothic" was used scornfully by the artists of the Renaissance to mean barbaric. Today it is a stylistic term, if not a badge of glory.

The sculpture, too, was subordinated in accord with the wishes of the Master of Chartres. At the old royal portal, with its majestic severe figures, the close Romanesque interrelationship of building and sculptural work can still be observed: the two are indissolubly bound, with the amorphous walls seeming almost to exude the sculpture, whether in the form of interlaced ornamentation or actual human forms.

Our Lady of Chartres is rich in portals—not

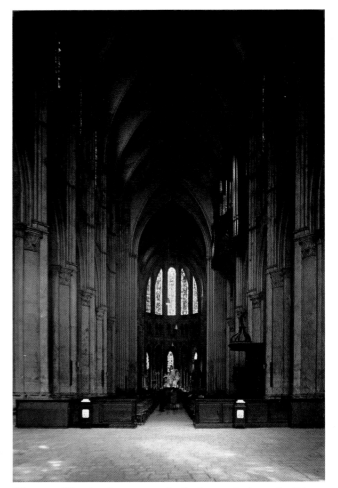

Kings, guilds, shopkeepers, and pilgrims united to rebuild their church in only three decades (1192–1220). By strictly systematizing a three-story structure and its component forms, the Master of Chartres created what was to be the prototype for the Gothic cathedral.

only the west end but also in the facades of the transepts. There the path that Gothic sculpture would take is clearly indicated. It wins its own individual existence and becomes independent, the relationship with the wall becoming looser, the figures more naturalistic. Later a new equilibrium between majesty and humanity would be attained at Reims, a balance that would come closer to the harmony of classical Greek figures than had anything created in all the intervening centuries.

Only simple floral capitals were tolerated in the church interior. The visitor may not linger before the portal sculpture, but its restrained symbolism is impressive, and merits the connoisseur's attention.

Everyone is immediately impressed by the stained-glass windows. To the theologians of the Middle Ages their unreachable light was especially close to the Divine and was the symbol of the Savior, whom St. John called the Light of the World. In these extraordinary windows pure artistic creation is joined to the church's concept of the Holy Jerusalem as the city of glass.

The technique of forming a picture out of colored panes joined by lead rods was not invented at Chartres. It had been perfected earlier, as can be seen in the cathedral at Augsburg. Unfortunately, nothing remains of the earliest, most experimental examples of stained glass, which is the most fragile of arts, in a very literal sense.

What the *vitrailleurs* at Chartres demonstrated with such extraordinary intensity is that the windows are the sole source of light in the church. When the full light of day streams into the Gothic space, the luminosity is almost blinding, and the sanctuary is filled with the music of color even as it is by the melody of the organ. Only a few churches have preserved their windows as completely as Chartres—the St. Chapelle in Paris and the cathedral of Leon, to name two. Along the aisles, the windows look like translucent walls of jeweled tapestrylike mosaics. By contrast the windows of the clerestory show stately figures of saints. "Notre Dame de la belle verrière" (Our Lady of the Beautiful Window) in the south ambulatory is one of the restored windows of the original cathedral. The king of France and his nobles as well as guilds and individual pilgrims made their contributions to the windows of Chartres, so the various trades are depicted in this celestial context, and donors are shown about their mundane activities. In the rose windows of the main nave and of the south and north transepts we can follow the development of tracery over three decades. But it is not the history of the art that is compelling—it is rather its effects, the unearthly impact of the light through the blues, reds, and golds.

The rigorous systematization of scholastic theology forms the very base of Chartres cathedral. It is a cosmos in which the parts yield to the whole and the whole is manifest in every detail. The entire Christian story is represented, from the Creation to the Last Judgment. Yet all of this would be mute were it not for the all-pervasive light.

BOURGES

The Cathedral of St. Etienne

The cathedral of Bourges is technically as old as Chartres. In 1195 the church leaders debated whether to reconstruct the old church, the victim, like Chartres, of fire, or to build a completely new structure.

Archbishop Henri de Sully (1183–1195) decided, in agreement with the cathedral chapter, in favor of the second option. His brother, formerly the Canon of Bourges, was Archbishop of Paris and building Notre Dame. So the obvious similarities between the two churches, especially their choir screens, is not surprising.

The choir of the new building overran the Gallo-Romanesque city wall, at which the old church terminated. The new building rose on uneven ground, a situation that gave Bourges a particular structural peculiarity: a Gothic sub-church in the form of a double-naved ambulatory. Unlike the crypts of the early and high Middle Ages, it was never intended for tombs or relics, being nothing more than the structural solution to a technical problem.

It was possible to begin the new building in the east without causing any disturbance to

religious services in the old cathedral, so first the choir was built, from east to west, over a period of twenty years. But the architect also began the new nave on the lateral walls of the old church and built from the outside toward the inside, so that the old building had to be abandoned only when the central nave pillars were begun. On the sides he used old elements (from about 1170) created to widen the original building but never used: two Late Romanesque portals of supreme perfection, comparable to those in the west facade of Chartres.

After the completion of the nave, the heightening of the towers was begun. But it was then discovered that the ground walls of the south tower were too weak. At a distance of several meters away the architect erected a mass of masonry the same size as the tower base. This served as a strong counterfort for the two pairs of flying buttresses that diverted the pressure of the heavy tower from its weak foundations.

The north tower, thought to be stable, collapsed on New Year's Eve, 1506. In its reconstruction, undertaken between 1508–1540, those

Bourges possesses stained-glass windows from the early Gothic period to the Renaissance. That in the Chapel of Jacques Coeur seems a translucent version of a Late Gothic panel painting.

who helped were exempted from the strict fasting of Holy Week, during which even butter was forbidden. And so the tower is known today as the Tour de Beurre, or Butter Tower. The south tower, left uncompleted and never hung with bells for fear it would sink further, became known as La Tour Sourde, the Deaf Tower.

Bourges and Chartres—how these two sisters of equal age differ! Chartres, on one hand, was built according to a system of hierarchical subordering and classification which was to become compulsory for the "classic" French cathedral. Bourges offered with similar completeness the alternative—integration rather than division. It might be said that Chartres was conceived from inside toward the outside and Bourges from the outside in. Chartres radiates, Bourges contains.

At Bourges, the nave overcomes everything else. But it also encloses the aisles; it is a single volume in which the pillars are placed like the trees in a wood and grow according to their proximity to the crossing. The unified space encompasses all. The master of Bourges even let the normally indispensable transept go by the wayside. It may be that this striving toward unity is also the reason why he did not cover the main nave with crossribbed vaults on a rectangular plan but instead gave priority to ancient, double-bay vaulting with sexpartite ribs. This allowed a slight variation in the thickness of the 670 foot (17 meter) high pillars of the middle nave, according to whether they supported a light midrib or an arch separating the naves. Such a subtle, almost unnoticeable fluctuation is one of the secrets of harmony and flexibility so surprising in this grand structure more than a hundred meters long.

The centuries have not been content to preserve the work of the Master of Bourges. Prominent families subscribed chapels between

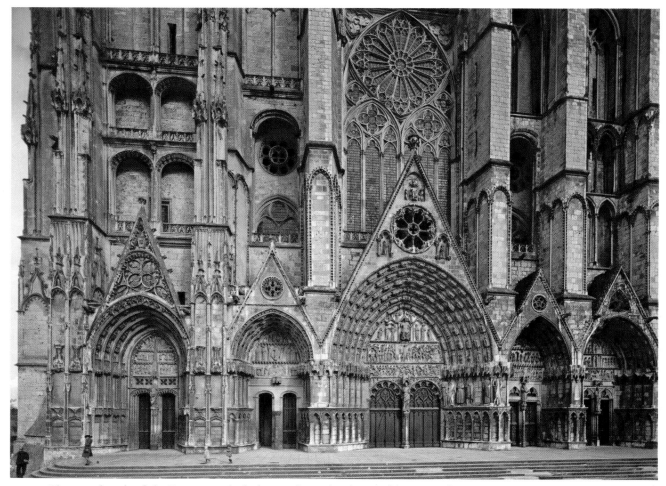

The west facade of the Bourges cathedral rises above the cluster of houses in the Old City. Its five portals correspond to the five naves of the interior. On the tympanum of the middle door is a representation of the Last Judgment, dividing mortal time from eternity.

Bourges cathedral is a magnificent encompassing whole, in which each individual detail yet prospers.

Bourges owes the wonderfully balanced space of its crypt to the technical necessity of compensating for the differing elevations of the sloped ground beneath it. In the background, the tomb of the Duke Jean de Berry.

the buttresses and assured themselves the right to interment there. One of these distinguished patrons was the Duke Jean de Berry, whose Book of Hours—"Les Très Riches Heures du Duc de Berry"—is singularly important in the history of manuscript illumination. In about 1390, through his court architect, Guy de Dammartin, he installed in the west facade the great west window reaching to the very crown of the nave. In that period Bourges, today so quiet and out of the mainstream, stood in the front lines of history. Until 1436 it was the seat of Charles VII, whom Joan of Arc had led to his coronation in Reims in 1429.

In Bourges cathedral one can study the whole development of stained glass. In the ambulatory the brilliantly glowing panes from the original building survive and bathe the space in bluish red light. Kaleidoscopic, with infinitesimal parts, they are truly glass mosaics. Of an altogether different type is the Late Gothic (about 1450) window in the Chapel of Jacques Coeur, chancellor to Charles VII, in the northern ambulatory: Mary is shown in dutiful contemplation and an angel in a billowing pluvial kneels before her. It is, in effect, a panel painting translated onto glass. The artist of this masterpiece is unknown, as are most of those of the Middle Ages. A hundred years later, in 1546, the story of the church's patron, Stephen, was represented by the glass-painter Jean Lécuyer in the window of the Capelle de Copin in the south aisle. In it we are confronted with buildings in Renaissance perspective, and the step to "paintings on glass" is not far away—the pure colors having given way to mixed tones and the panes having become larger.

Yet one always comes back to the wonderful central space of Bourges and perhaps begins to understand why medieval church construction was considered a service to God, a sacred duty, an act of faith.

ALBI

The Cathedral of St. Cecile

Albi is a red city. The soil is red; the houses and bridges are red. The cathedral, too, is red, and even the Tarn River not infrequently takes on the color of brick.

To anyone who ventures into the city on a stormy afternoon, the mass of the cathedral seems to press up against the tangle of houses in the Old City like a giant warship run aground. It is like a petrified memorial to the bloody Albigensian wars, with their pitiless persecution of heretics, which raged here in the thirteenth century. When Bernard de Castanet took possession of the old cathedral in 1277 and read his first mass as bishop in the scarcely century-old but severely damaged church, the struggle had almost ended. But there were things he chose not to forget, and Bernard himself became a passionate persecutor of real and supposed unbelievers, on whose earthly possessions he had certain designs. He thus accrued in the city and country under his authority not only wealth but enemies.

It is not surprising that the cathedral too—whose building Bernard initiated, in direct agreement with the chapter and citizenry, on August 5, 1282—had the outward appearance of a repulsing fortress, with the episcopal castle surrounded by both wall and moat. The relationship between bishop, city, and chapter in Albi stretched back over centuries, as noted by a witness of the fifteenth century: "Although Albi has a cathedral, its inhabitants have never lived in peace with their lord."

Today, rampart and moat can be seen at only a few places on the city side. Elsewhere the church is surrounded by the empty expanse of a tarred piazza. But there still stands, in all its massiveness, an erratic block, the cathedral. It is of a piece, erected in a century and completed about 1390. It rises from a strict rectilinear pedestal like the hull of a crude ship, with a unified mass of walls. Not angular or pointed, but with its brick walls strengthened by semicircular projections, the cathedral had no exterior ornamentation. The tower dominates, climbing up the west side out of the weighty cylinders and three-quarter-round buttressing. The high windows almost seem cut out and are decorated

19

As aloof as a fortress, the cathedral seems to weigh down
on the city. When construction was begun in 1282
memories of the bloody Albigensian wars were still fresh.
In the foreground, the episcopal palace, which looks like
the military guardian of the cathedral.

with simple, restrained tracery. There is no graduation of the naves, neither crossing nor transept. The walls ascend in one sweep right up to the roof and enclose the whole. Only in the vicinity of the choir are the pillars and windows, imperceptibly, more closely placed.

The interior is a colossal room without intermediary supports, spanned by sinewy, ribbed vaults, totally exposed. The projecting pilasters in the interior correspond to the round turrets on the outside; these too are without ornament, simple in contour, marked uniquely by the design of the bricks, which sometimes are laid transversely, sometimes obliquely Only on the west wall does the rhythm change. If the interior is otherwise determined completely by line and surface, here the easterly round pillars of the towers come visibly, voluminously, to light and emphasize undisguisedly the mass of the edifice.

The cathedral of Albi, so different from its French sisters, became, with its straightforward form and unique nave, the model for a whole array of churches in Languedoc. It is not the details and embellishments of the design which command one's admiration, but its homogeneous, grand-scale conception, foregoing all excesses. Limited forms and elements have here triumphed in a great work of art. The linear clarity of the broad church space contrasts strikingly with the massive modeling of the exterior. What is outside closure and volume becomes space and line within.

Inside, the vaults swell out like blue sails. For the entire building of the thirteenth and fourteenth centuries was frescoed between 1509 and 1514, creating an interior garment of great uniformity. The basic color is a luminous blue graced by figures and ornamentation in gray and gold. Colorful marbles and designs define the supporting columns and exterior walls. The ceiling paintings follow no strict plan: one can see Christ and the Apostles, saints, prophets, scenes out of the life of Jesus, Christian parables, allegories of the virtues and the arts, as well as the coat of arms of Bishop Louis II of Amboise, the donor for all the pictorial decoration. And for all posterity, its creator has identified himself twice in the south choir chapels: "Joan Franciscus Donnela, pictor italus de Carpa Fecit," and the dates 1509–1514. Rather strangely, this master, whose work speaks for his skill, is otherwise unknown in the history of art. But he did the service of ushering in the new art of the Renaissance to all of southern France.

Louis I of Amboise, uncle and predecessor of the patron of the ceiling, had the rood and choir screen fashioned in the rich Late Gothic style. Admittedly our modern sensibility might object that the installation of this screening bisects the room and detracts from its overall effect. But we must realize that the Middle Ages did not regard the church space as an artistic monument but rather saw it as a setting for all-important holy offices and as a priceless shell to be filled with precious and holy utensils.

What is most remarkable at Albi is that within the wide church there is a second one: the choir enclosure and screens, which occupy the entire eastern half of the church. The smaller space is similar to the whole in layout but so different in effect! The major building, an imposing fortress of red brick on the outside and uniform, severe, and spare inside, is by all accounts ascetic. In contrast, the filigree of white stone in the mini-

The vaults, with their blue-gold Renaissance paintings, span the wide cathedral like sails.

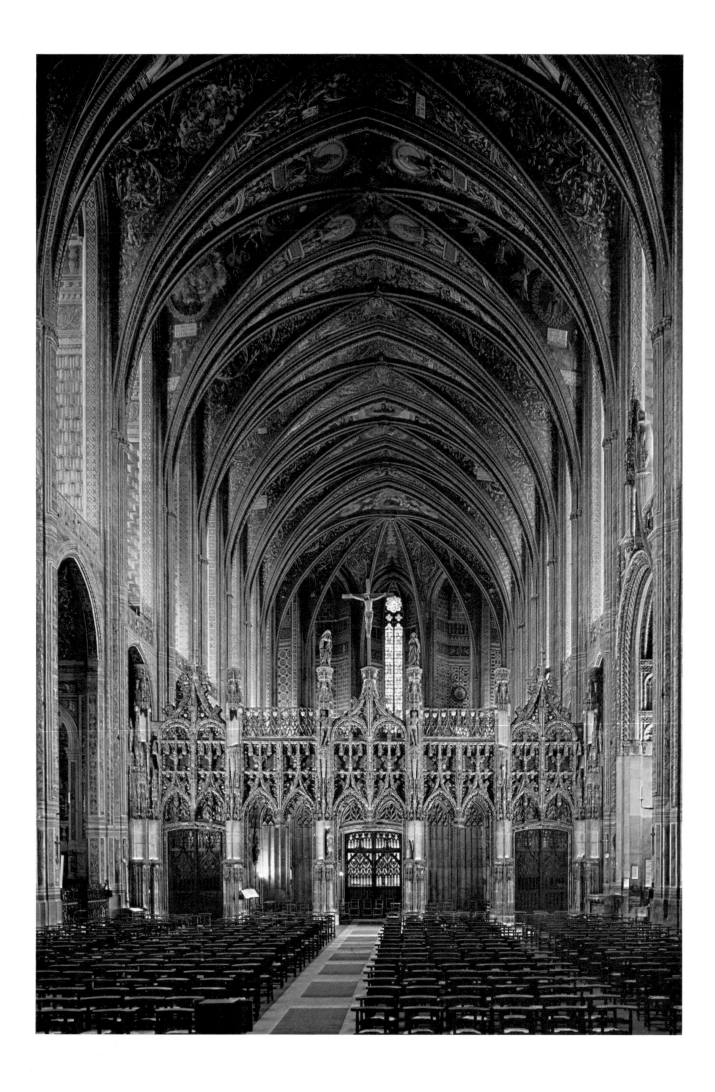

Cardinal Richelieu had a piece of the filigreed choir stall ornamentation brought to him personally to convince him that it was truly stone. Prophets stand on the outer side of the stalls, apostles on the inside.

ature church is all decoration and elegance. The work is of such fineness that it appears to be made more out of jewels than of stone; Cardinal Richelieu had a sample brought to him in 1629 to convince himself that his eye was not deceived by painted plaster. The architecture of the main church can be described quickly and simply without many details going unmentioned. A description of the small sanctuary, however, must run aground at its profusion of forms, at its luxuriant richness. There is nothing to do but to go to Albi and see it for oneself.

On the outside every pillar bears the figure of a prophet, the framework being, as it were, the Old Testament thirsting after salvation and fulfillment. At the altar, inside the wonderfully carved Late Gothic gates, one sees the apostles gathered around the Virgin Mary. In the rear the choir stalls are crowned with angels, which stand out brightly before an alternating red and blue ground and hold up scrolls in an everlasting song of praise. But these figures, arrayed in white robes with abundant, heavily falling folds and probably created by Burgundian masters, do not project, for all their beauty, an aura of joy. Quiet thought, suffering, and modesty are readable in the faces, and Emile Male's observation about the art of 1500 is especially applicable: "It seems that the key Christian word is no more Love but Suffering." Who would have expected this bitter strain amidst such alabaster splendor?

The screen and choir at Albi are exceptional rarities, for only a few works of the type have survived the centuries. What survived the Reformation fell to the baroque craze for building and—in France above all—to the destructive fury of the Revolution. There is no statuary on the screen; it was destroyed in 1794.

Going back into the nave, we find the west

The only ornamentation on the brick red body of the church is the stone
baldachin above the entrance, adorned with elaborate Late Gothic decoration.

wall with its great organ. The nine-rank console is counted among the largest in all France. It is the work of Christophe Moucherel and was built in 1734–1736. Originally an instrument with five manuals and forty-three registers, it has since been rebuilt and enlarged many times. Beneath the organ tribune, painted on the thin plaster of the tower pillar, is a monumental Last Judgment from the fifteenth century. The central group of figures has been missing since the seventeenth century; at that time a large opening was made in the wall in order to create a passage to the lowest tower chapel.

The tower itself—raised in the fourteenth century to just above the height of the church roof—was completed as a result of a testamentary decree by Bishop Louis I of Amboise. Over the massive base a two-storied octagonal construction with broad acoustic arcades was built, to which the Late Gothic period, almost bashfully, attempted to add several pinnacles.

But the tower cannot rival the round, chimney-like turrets with winding staircases which rise out of the lower floors and ultimately surpass it in height.

The Late Gothic asserted itself a last time on the great portal baldachin, which looks as if the ornament-mad master of the choir screen carried his work outside the giant tabernacle. Its columns recapitulate the round pillars of the external buttressing, but the adornment virtually spills over, like a mass of liquid porcelain that has partly congealed and crystallized over the vault with several rivulets streaming almost to the ground.

Until modern times nothing on the church exterior matched this monumental decoration. Only in the nineteenth century were the bare walls crowned by a fluted frieze, copied from the tower, and a balustrade. But even this cosmetic operation has taken nothing from the austere grandeur of this fortress cathedral.

VENICE

The Basilica of San Marco

San Marco is a golden vessel. It is not the reserved eleventh-century architecture that impresses, but the unimaginably golden scintillation. San Marco is rightly called the Golden Basilica, for, like precious coverings, golden mosaics grace every part of the building not occupied by jeweled columns or paneling. All the angles in this relatively severe building become supple transitions, and one thinks that the room has been hollowed out of a great, golden crag and not—as is the case—ordained from simple brick. Yet San Marco is smaller than many a city parish church, and this is not by accident.

The present-day patriarchal basilica first rose to the rank of cathedral in the twelfth century when the Patriarch von Grado transferred his see here. Later the might and importance of the city grew. The basilica was built as the chapel of the Doges, whose palace adjoins it, and as a shrine for relics of the apostle and evangelist Mark, which were brought here from Alexandria in the ninth century. In time the church became the center of all Venetian worship. The present-day structure is successor to a smaller one of the Carolingian period, which was also cruciform, after the model of the Apostle's Church in Constantinople. It has been suggested that Byzantine builders erected this structure so unique in the West; yet the engineering of the walls is clearly Italian, and only the model for the architecture is Eastern. San Marco itself became the model for the cathedral at Perigueux.

The church is not a long building with nave and choir, but rather a Greek cross in plan, based on the square and circle, with four arms of equal length. Above the crossing and over each arm of the cross swell domes separated by broad bands of stone and supported by square, cross-shaped pillars. Only the apse in the east and the narthex at the western end give the building a clear "direction."

At the side of the domes, beneath cradle vaults, are areas like aisles. Pillars are stretched between these and the central nave and seem to have no real purpose. They once carried galleries. Then, at the beginning of the twelfth century, the golden mosaic carpet began to spread in darkening exuberance over most of the win-

The four bronze horses on the facade once adorned the riding school in Constantinople; the Doge Enrico Dandolo brought them back to Venice as plunder. They represent the only surviving quadriga of ancient times.

dows. Today these orphaned columns are an essential part of the mystical impression one receives of San Marco. One can wander, as if on catwalks, over the fixed ridges of its arcades, confronted by saintly figures emerging from the gold background.

The mosaic is an ancient decorative technique. In a freshly applied, still-soft layer of mortar, varicolored or gilded stones are closely emplaced so that only their surfaces are visible. The unevenness of the small stones and their different textures give the mosaic a play of light that no painting could achieve. The effect is all the more mysterious in a darkened room with an indirect source of light. In the Middle Ages the numerous small windows in the side walls were closed and the faces of the main nave and transept in the south and west were opened almost completely so that reflected light from a seemingly unknown source could break into the vaults. It is such an impressive phenomenon that even in restorations during the illusionistic baroque period the traditional gold ground was preserved—an indication that earlier ages appreciated what was at hand and did not necessarily rebuild uncompromisingly in their own styles.

The layout of the church is radial. In the vestibule or porch is a thirteenth-century representation of the story of the Nine Tribes of the Old Testament. Entering the church itself, one sees in the three main domes, beginning in the east with the Exaltation of the Savior by the evangelists and prophets under the tutelage of Mary, the Ascension, and the Pentecost. The Ascension cupola is stylistically the oldest—its precursors are the early Christian mosaics of Ravenna ("The Baptizing of the Orthodox")— but was actually created about 1200 and so is more recent than the other two (about 1150).

Like the palace of an oriental fairy tale, the front of San Marco is ever promising and never completely revealing. Over the centuries the simple brick walls of this Doges' palace chapel of the High Middle Ages have been dressed out with columns and rare stones brought home by Venetian galleys.

The domes of the transept are dedicated to John the Evangelist and St. Leonhard and are thus clearly subordinated to the main theme. The mosaic decoration of the basilica was completed toward the end of the thirteenth century but was constantly being repaired, restored, or in part replaced.

Today we discriminate between two zones of the building: the lower area up to the height of the pillared arcades, where walls and pillars are arrayed with marble plaques; and an upper region reserved as a celestial golden ground for the Savior and the saints.

The lower part is worth a closer look, for here too San Marco distinguishes itself from other churches. The sculpture—in so many other buildings tied in with distinct architectural rapports and closely related to the interior structure—here follows ideas of another order. There are, of course, the capitals of the pillars. But otherwise reliefs seem to be fit in at random like precious stones in the frame of the marble wall. The Venetians seem never to have forgotten their cathedral during their travels and to have brought home solemn gifts as homage to their protective patron. We find plaques from valuable Mediterranean quarries on the balustrades of the two lecterns flanking the choir entrance and on the banisters of the walkways.

The choir, because of the crypt lying beneath it, is elevated and separated from the congregational nave, according to early Christian tradition. On the balconies supported by pillars stand the bronze figures of the Crucifix and the apostles, completed in 1394 by Jacopello and Pier-Paolo Dalle Masegne.

The high altar stands free in the choir beneath a priceless baldachin of various marbles. A century ago the relics of St. Mark that previously resided in the crypt were transferred to the altar,

a late reprise of a practice of the late Middle Ages whereby bones of saints were removed from their crypts and made observable inside sumptuous shrines. Behind the high altar the gold of the mosaics presents a still more striking luster.

The Pala d'Oro, or Golden Retable, is one of the glories of San Marco. It shows the influence of both Eastern and Western art so characteristic of the whole church. Ordered in Byzantium in 976 for San Marco, it was originally an *antependium*, or a hanging for the altar front. Renovations and remodeling in 1105, 1209, and 1342 widened the original piece and the panel became an altar fixture. The entire development of Byzantine enamel painting can be read in its 180 images. The periphery, with its keep arches and pinnacles, is an Italian work of the fourteenth century and is signed by its creator, Johannes Bonensegna. It is resplendent with hundreds of pearls and brilliants, so that the innocent observer is overwhelmed by the unsurpassed treasure.

In the Middle Ages the exterior facades of plain masonry stood in an ever more pronounced contrast to the growing splendor of the interior and could soon no longer satisfy the esthetic needs of the sea-ruling Venetian republic. After the Fourth Crusade of 1204 the ships returned from conquered Byzantium with great quantities of pillars and decorative stonework, which were used to adorn San Marco. And so the church developed, in place of

---

Golden mosaics give the room a close, mystical atmosphere not found in any other Western church. This view from the west gallery shows three of the building's five domes.

restraint, a kind of vivid architectural chiaroscuro. The four bronze horses above the main entrance are also booty from Byzantium. The Doge Enrico Dandolo took them out of the riding school of the imperial city, to which they were apparently brought by Constantine. In fact, this is the only ancient quadriga to survive to our day. Petrarch himself celebrated the horses' naturalness and beauty, believing he could hear their very neighing and stamping.

The flat canopies of the domes seem modest in contrast to the new splendor of the lower parts. This lack was overcome by high, lead-covered bell casings over wooden scaffolding, additions which helped make the church the fantastic temple it remains.

One can only hope that San Marco will endure, for Venice is endangered. The land is sinking, moisture is climbing up the city's old walls, and residents leave for firmer ground. An emergency campaign by UNESCO has set as one of its goals the preservation of this jewel of the Occident. Measures to be taken include cleaning and restoring the buildings and improving social conditions, tasks which in the current crisis will pose extraordinary problems.

The Pala d'Oro reflects the tension between Eastern and Western art, an ambivalence characteristic of Venice. Its oldest parts go back to 976 and were made in Byzantium. It owes its present-day form to an Italian artist of the fourteenth century who fashioned the retable out of an antependium.

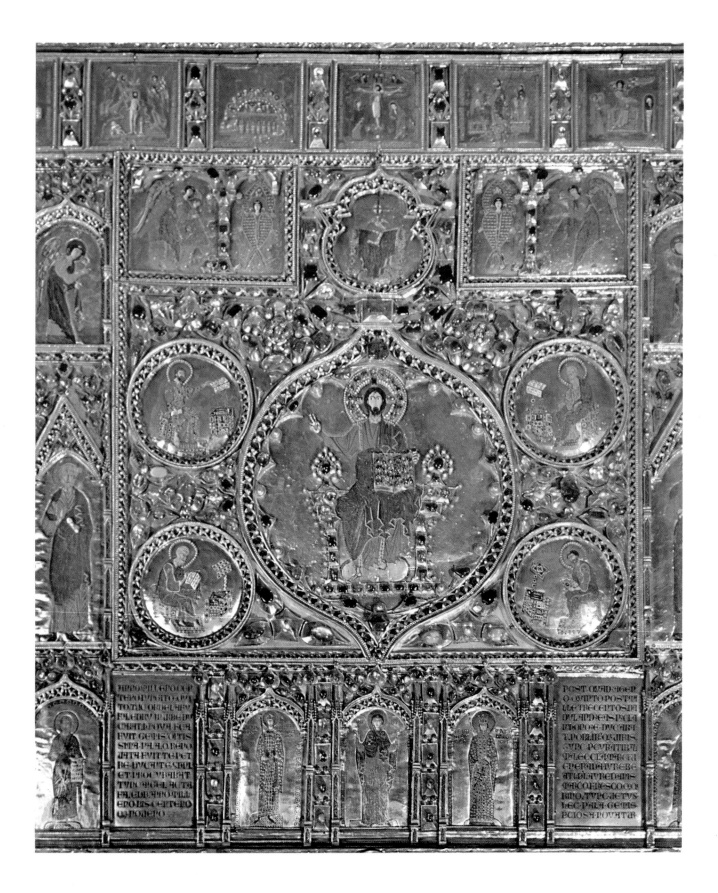

FLORENCE

The Cathedral of
Santa Maria del Fiore

So many illustrious names are associated with this cathedral: Arnolfo di Cambio, Talenti, Ghiberti, Giotto, Brunelleschi, Nanni di Banco, Luca della Robbia, Paolo Uccello, Donatello, Michelangelo, Bandinelli, and Vasari.

One could envison a church overflowing with masterpieces, a temple of the muses, since so many famous artists lent their talents and energies to it. But such is not the case. We are struck by the plainness of the interior of Santa Maria del Fiore. Only the floor, made of different marbles, reminds us of the light, playful exterior. Otherwise, the interior of the church is decorated with only the simple brownish stone of the pillars, pedestals, and the ribbed vaults alternating with the light-colored wall. Certainly renovation has had its purifying effect here too. But the overriding ambience of the room is tranquility, like the imperturbable soul of the great city.

In Santa Maria del Fiore, two radically different structural parts are united without discord: the slender-membered, hall-like nave, in which Gothic creative will and classical sen-

sibilities meet, and the central massiveness of the choir. That Brunelleschi's dome is given far more space in art-history books than is the nave, is understandable in view of its ingenious construction. But we must realize that the cathedral lives, architecturally speaking, in the contrast of the two elements.

From the rooftops of the city, the great Duomo seems to be the pivotal point of the whole region. Even the 325 foot (100 meter) high campanile, standing free next to the west front, is subordinated to it—not slavishly, to be sure, but as an independent form inextricably linked with the dome through their common garb of polychromed marble. This same patina also covers the walls of the nave and the other

---

With his mighty cathedral dome, Filippo Brunelleschi created the definitive model for dome construction of the Renaissance and gave Florence a focal point, around which the city seems to turn as if about a hub.

34

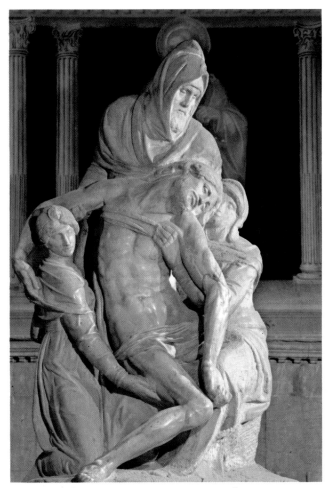

Michelangelo took up the subject of the Pietà twice. In his youth he rendered it in calm, stately beauty (Pietà of St. Peter's). This sculpture, planned for his own tomb but never finished (1547–1555), captures the moment of the Deposition in all its pathos.

octagonal structure facing the front, the baptistery, or christening church of the cathedral.

The baptistery has its structural antecedents in the early Middle Ages, and in its interior reveals the ornamentation we expected in the main church nave. Fourteen distinctive granite pillars with splendid capitals dominate. When the cupola lighting fades, one feels he is in a great mausoleum whose form is only barely perceptible in the dim, shadowy light. The chief light sources are the portals, hung with the famous bronze doors of Andrea Pisano (south door, made 1330–1336) and Lorenzo Ghiberti (north door, made 1403–1424; and east door or "Gate of Paradise," made 1425–1452). One wonders how visitors of earlier times could have seen the glittering mosaics of the eight-sided cupola without electric spotlights to illuminate them. But here, too, the artist did not create his work solely to please the floor-bound viewer but chiefly to serve the glory of God.

It is here that the anti-pope John XXIII found rest, having been dethroned by the Council of Constance. *"Joanes Quondam Papa"* (John, Once Pope) is inscribed on his wall sepulcher. The grave has its place in art history as the first baldachin memorial of the Renaissance, created by Donatello and Michelozzo about 1425.

In contrast to the mystical half-light of the interior is the crystalline clarity of the outer structure. Protecting the sharp-edged octagonal construction is an equally linear, closely hewn tent roof.

The cathedral to which the baptistery was once annexed, Santa Reparata, stands no more. The Romanesque building was significantly smaller than the present church, begun by Arnolfo di Cambio in 1296, and was more closely incorporated with the baptistery than this one. But the chief architect was really the city itself, and responsibility for specific aspects of the construction was assumed by the various guilds—the Campanile, for example, was the province of the wool weavers. Accordingly, building decisions and changes in plans were not matters for individual consideration but were the result of competitions and awarded commissions.

Arnolfo began his work with the flanking walls on the west, and the minutely articulated rhythm of his bays is still recognizable in the western part on the outer side. Before Francesco Talenti expanded the plan to its present-day size, Giotto had become the cathedral's master builder (in 1334) and had begun the bell tower; but he completed only the pedestal. Andrea Pisano continued the work, and Talenti completed the upper stories with ever-higher levels and widened bays. The steeple originally planned was never executed.

Vasari's biography of Filippo Brunelleschi conveys the full suspense of the erecting of the dome. A unique risk, at once enticing and frightening, it was mastered only by the summoning of all the architect's energies, discernment, and courage. In a time when the builder's art was still largely anonymous north of the Alps, Italy produced in Brunelleschi a confident personality to create a work technically and esthetically unprecedented. To be sure, it was not Brunelleschi who determined the diameter of the dome. The encompassing walls of the central building counted much more and a cupola was foreseen, though no one knew how the clear breadth of 133 feet (41 meters) could be spanned. Out of a civic competition of builders from all Europe, there emerged no single winner. As a result the designs of Brunelleschi and Ghiberti were kept and ultimately both were put in charge of the work.

It was Brunelleschi who eventually finished

In the main church space, the broad, finely articulated, hall-like nave contrasts with the soaring, strong-walled central area of the choir, arched over by the dome.

the project alone. He had studied the dome engineering of ancient buildings, especially that of the Pantheon, and also knew the medieval solution to the baptistery of his home city. The dome of the Florence cathedral, justly extolled as the "dowry of the Renaissance," followed Gothic building principles. The ground plan of an octagon was dictated by the existing walls. Above these the master arched an immense shell, without center-framings, in the form of a Gothic-arched, ribbed vault. The Roman casting technique was precluded not only by the ground plan but also by the weak substructure. Brunelleschi developed not only the system for the dome but the details, the specially formed bricks and the braces between the two cupola walls. As a parallel to the inner dome shell he constructed an outer one for protection from the weather, a principle that was to be adopted many times over in later centuries.

The building activity must have been a colorful spectacle. Since it was an increasing nuisance for the laborers to descend from the scaffolding as the building height grew, shops and kitchens were erected on the armature itself. Nor did Brunelleschi forget to install hooks in the vaults to which the painters' scaffolding could later be affixed. Vasari, his biographer, is said to have used them. As the crowning touch, the master designed the wonderfully graceful lantern, whose intricate design reveals that its creator was originally a goldsmith.

Brunelleschi was never to see his work com-pleted. At its consecration in 1436, Santa Maria del Fiore was the largest church in all Italy. Rival city republics such as Bologna and Siena wanted to compete, with yet more colossal structures, but all of their attempts remained fragments.

Michelangelo's contribution to Santa Maria del Fiore was originally intended for the tomb of the artist. It was a late work with a theme that had preoccupied the sculptor even in his youth: the Pietà. Whereas the St. Peter's group portrays the young mother detached from reality and immediacy calmly holding the body of her son, the Florentine group is remarkable for its immediate sense of tragedy and humanity. It captures the moment of the Descent from the Cross, with Mary receiving the flaccid body of Jesus from Nicodemus. The suffering Christ is represented almost upright, his right leg brought back beneath the collapsing burden. Around this central body, the only one finished, Michelangelo grouped the other figures into a three-cornered supporting composition. The work came to a standstill after the left leg of Christ broke off during the sculpting, and though Michelangelo resumed the work in 1547, he smashed it in 1555, feeling he could not realize his conception. One of his pupils, Tiberio Calcagni, reassembled the pieces and tried to carry on, but fortunately he soon lost heart. The Florence Pietà now seems like Schubert's Unfinished Symphony, complete and superb even as a fragment.

On the balustrade of the Singer's Tribune (commissioned 1431), Donatello represented angelic children frolicking in an irrepressible round dance. The contrast between the white marble figures and the mosaiced foreground and background creates an ambulatory within which the dance flows.

ROME

The Basilica of St. Peter

Approaching St. Peter's from the east one might say that he passes the stages of its construction in reverse. Bernini's colonnades, which receive pilgrims like open arms and lead the grand design (built 1656–1657). A quarter of a century earlier Carlo Maderna had completed the broad entrance facades after building the nave (1607–1614). Only when we are beneath the dome are we in the earliest part of the building, which is associated with Donato Bramante (1444–1514) and Michelangelo Buonarroti (1475–1564). Here the original conception becomes obvious. Bramante had conceived a centralized structure, a great dome over four pillars, between which would radiate barrel-vaulted naves, linked through squared cupolated chambers in the spandrels.

Under Michelangelo, who took over construction in 1546, the character of the architecture evolved from Bramante's aim, the finesse and multiplicity of elements of the High Renaissance, to an integrated design wherein space and external form almost danced out of an imaginary wall like sculpture out of a stone block. Michelangelo abandoned Bramante's plan for partitioned and terraced annexes in favor of the linear, crystalline legibility of planes and less precise, often broken, contours. Instead of two bays, each nave now has only one, framed by mighty pairs of pillars. Yet the basic idea of the central building remains, with a dominating dome as a crown. It had hardly been completed when Pope Paul V (1605–1626) decided that the eastern arm should be lengthened to become the main nave because the directionless, centralized architectural approach did not conform to the new dictates of the Council of Trent and because, more importantly, the new building occupied only a part of the holy precinct on which the old basilica, established by the Emperor Constantine in the fourth century, had stood.

The visitor once arrived at the colonnades of Bernini through narrow alleys. Today they are reached by the broad Via della Conciliazione. But the modern piazza still allows the pedestrian to escape the city traffic for another world. The wide arena unfolds in quiet majesty, framed by four ranks of colonnades which formally exclude the city and its tangle of houses. Even the Vatican Palace itself seems to have set-

In order to cover the entire side of the old basilica of St. Peter's, and to satisfy
the demands of the Council of Trent, Pope Paul V had Carlo Maderna lengthen
the east arm of the main structure. When seen from the piazza fronting St.
Peter's the baroque facade hides the dome.

tled its walls about it in spacious luxury. An Egyptian obelisk marks the middle of the round expanse, and two fountains rise from the focal points of the ellipse.

One can proceed directly across the piazza to the main portal. We prefer to follow the colonnades and to enjoy, as if in review, the changing prospect, always framed by pillars. Taxis, fountains, the Vatican Palace, pilgrims on a picnic, a monsignor with broad-brimmed hat—all serve as a makeshift scale for assessing the dimensions of the columns.

In the open again, we see Maderna's facade unfolding in all of its monumental weight, an effect only heightened by the funnel of closed corridors that block it before it flows out into a circle of colonnades.

To see the dome in its proper perspective we must wend our way to the western end of the church where the effect of Michelangelo's sculptural architecture is not obstructed, and the substructure and cupola can be recognized as masterpieces of complementary forms. The interplay is different from that at the Florence cathedral, where the always-manifest octagonal form gradually dominates the outbuildings and buttresses. At St. Peter's the exterior scarcely indicates the inner organization of the building, with its many partitions, mighty pillars, heavy attic, and pedestal for the dome. Like a crown, the dome seems to float in a harmonious current of circling horizontals, over double columns and ribs, up to the top of the cross.

Now to go inside: the great outer staircase high over the porch is a church in itself! Five portals lead from it into the church interior. On the middle portal Maderna reused the bronze wings that the pope of the Council of Basel, Eugene IV (1431–1447), had given to the Flor-

entine Filarete; a part of the old basilica lives on even more magnificently in the new one.

St. Peter's does not flaunt its dimensions. But as one begins to move about inside it the arches and pilasters glide above in a solemn grandeur. Light streams forward into the nave from three elevated windows. The western bay is distinguished by its narrowness and lack of windows; it is an arm of the original central building, left intact by Maderna except for a lengthening of the apse.

The atmosphere in the nave is cool; it awakens, however, when troops of pilgrims fill it. In the side naves the atmosphere is more compact, the light uncertain, the colors ranging from cool gray to reddish marble. Although the great dome beckons, we make our way to the right lateral nave and again walk from new to old. Chapels line the nave. We pause behind these, near the Porta Sancta, which is opened only in feast years—every twenty-five years, 1975 being the most recent occasion.

Here is one of the masterpieces of religious art, Michelangelo's *Pietà*. For twenty-five years he worked on it for the Petronilla Chapel, an early Christian rotunda in the south transept of the old church, and he signed it as his work. We find no trace here of the tragic urgency of the Florence *Pietà*. All is restful. A young mother serenely bears the body of her son, who lies spare and lifeless against the folded garment on her knees. Faultlessly smooth, the *Pietà* is a symbol of supreme Christian faith.

As we emerge from the chapel, the middle nave spreads before us like a wide piazza. We are bound for the confessio beneath the great dome—the structural center of the old and new basilicas and the very reason for there being a church here. This is thought to be the place St.

From the Vatican gardens, the original feeling of Michelangelo's central structure can still be appreciated. The dome seems to hover above the massive supporting building.

While the central nave has a feeling of great distances and magnificence, the soft colors and articulation of the side naves almost make the visitor forget the enormity of the building.

The dome soars weightlessly above the tomb of St. Peter, at the very center and root of the largest church in the world. Excavations have confirmed that the apostle probably was buried at this spot. The site has been revered from earliest times.

Peter was buried after his crucifixion. Archeological investigations conducted under Pope Pius XII concluded that the emperor Constantine erected his basilica over a Roman cemetery. The earth had been evened out to make a second-century tomb, found to the east of a red-plastered wall, the center of a large apse. Constantine was convinced that the tomb contained the remains of the archapostle, and archeologists' findings seem to confirm his belief. It is impressive to see that fickle man has kept this place in such honor through almost two thousand years—that the old has not been swept aside, but enhanced. A person descending to the crypt today can still see the marble covering Constantine gave the back wall or "Red Wall," which was to become the early medieval altar. On the west side is a niche containing the pallium, hollowed out as the *memoria* to St. Peter. In succeeding generations the church became a great mausoleum, full of the tombs of popes, emperors, and kings. Their memorials are documents that signal the unbroken tradition of the old basilica. Even the form of the mighty pillars of the great baldachino altar of Lorenzo Bernini echo antiquity, for the columns of the choir stalls in the old church had spiraled shafts. Today they frame the recesses above the balconies of the great pillars beneath the dome. The view upward remains unforgettable: like bright peals of trumpets, the light falls in rays through the high window of the drum and gilds whatever it meets.

The dome soars with unbelievable lightness from the heavy cornice supported by a crown of decorative consoles. What we experience outside as a dynamic sculpture is almost incorporeally delicate inside. A sense of motion pervades the space above the windows and their alternating gable forms. In the central baldachin, Bernini created a sculpture perfectly congenial to this most plastic room. With every change of his vantage point, the visitor experiences ever-new perspectives. Bernini not only surrounded the grave of St. Peter with splendor, he made the memorial basilica a throne room of the apostleprince. In the central apse, a tour de force of baroque illusion, stands the "Cathedra Petri." Through the baldachin, its golden rays break into the church space. If one advances further, between the baldachin and aureola, sculptures of the four church fathers, surrounding the throne, come clearly into view.

The baldachin symbolizes the architectural unity of the approaching Renaissance, for it is three-dimensionally centralized, and the Cathedra represents the glorious terminal of one of the arms of the cross. Yet the entire effect is not simply ornamental. The splendid throne reaffirms a chair which was already venerated in the Middle Ages, a seat upon which, tradition has it, Peter once sat in the house of the Senator Pudens. Thus the apse is actually a monumental reliquary, and his commission enabled Bernini to realize a wish he had nurtured since youth: to build in the apse of St. Peter's a throne to the glory of God.

Among the patron popes whose commissions

Bernini realized his lifelong wish to build a throne to St. Peter in the apse. The seat, supported by figures of the four church fathers, contains an early medieval armchair, the "Cathedra Petri," long believed to have been used by the apostle. The yellow glass work at the center of the Gloriole was subsequently adopted in many baroque churches.

to artists culminated in the glory of the Vatican basilica are Julius II, who supported Bramante, Paul III, who named Michelangelo architect, and Urban VIII, who commissioned Bernini for the baldachin and the Cathedra. To fully appreciate St. Peter's, it is important to remember what a unique, peerless role this cathedral has played in the history of Christianity.

CHUR

The Cathedral of Mariä Himmelfahrt

This is one of the most historic sites in all of Switzerland. Chur was spared by the Alemannic assaults, and the ancient administration endured until it was dissolved in the eighth century by the Franks. A bishop of Chur is mentioned as early as 451, and in the seventh and eighth centuries the family of the Victorides united the offices of bishop and "president." The testament of the last Victoride, Tello (765), gives us a picture of a well-honed and advanced ecclesiastical organization.

The present-day cathedral had two predecessors on the same site, the first from the period before 450; the second apparently from Tello's time. Parts of the Vintschgauer marble choir stalls from the latter church have been preserved.

Heavy clustered lapidary piers support the tripartite nave at Chur with cupolaed vaults and bandlike ribs, and the main nave continues east to the square choir and thin, rectangular altar house, or chancel. A Cistercian bishop, Adalgott (1151–1160), commissioned the building, which was consecrated in 1178. The ground plan has no right angles but follows the slope of the rock on which the church and episcopal palace, entered by a steep ramp through a gated tower, fitly repose.

In addition to the characteristic ornamentation of the entwined pretzel-like "pleated ribbons," there are antique motifs such as grapes and beribboned bouquets of flowers. The Carolingian high altar was refurbished in late Romanesque times. The old altar platform, with its elevated margin in the ancient tradition, may have been used to celebrate mass in the first cathedral. Over the altar block, however, rises the greatest and most important carved altar in Switzerland, the six-year labor of Jakob Ruess of Ravensburg (1492).

One must contemplate the altar carefully. The chestlike shrine is furnished with a Late Gothic net vault and opens to the front in three poised ogival arches. On the gilded back wall eight small angels hold a curtain in front of which the Chur patrons appear; at the middle of the rapt group sits Mary. Standing at her side are St. Ursula and St. Emerita, and on the outside are St.

49

Chur cathedral is one of the smallest cathedrals north of the Alps, but also one of the richest in traditions. In its Late Romanesque interior it harbors artifacts from early medieval to modern times.

Lucius as a king and St. Florinus. Each figure seems self-absorbed and serene, and the Christ Child's tentative play with the offered apple hardly disturbs the esthetic calm. The group is seen only on Sundays, when the wings of the shrine are opened. On the wings themselves four saints are depicted: the donors of the monasteries at St. Gall and Disentis, who face one another and seem to symbolize their common vocation. On the exterior of the closed leaves are depictions of the Nativity and the Adoration of the Magi. The paintings are attributed to Master Michael, who perhaps came from Hans Huber's circle out of Feldkirch. On feast days the altar emanates a golden radiance, on ordinary days the more discrete aura of the painting. But in the pedestal, or predella, three scenes from the Passion are always visible. A further look reveals a surprise on the back of the retable; it, too, bears sculptures, the continuation of the Passion. The multifigured Crucifixion takes up the greatest space with the three crosses of Christ and the thieves. The crown of the shrine, a filigreed framework of Gothic turrets and baldachins, is always visible. There the ascended mother of Christ is crowned by the tribune God as six apostles stand meditatively nearby. The End of the World is represented at the very top of the crown where John and Mary plead for grace before the Lord.

Back in the nave we climb to the Gothic choir stalls and the tabernacle of Claus von Feldkirch (1484). The choir is strongly elevated, for

The high altar, by Jakob Ruess of Ravensburg (1492). Only on feast days, when the wings of the shrine are opened, can the coruscating golden figures of its saints be observed. The leaves are usually kept closed and show their painted outer sides.

This marble plaque with characteristic plaiting once belonged to an early medieval choir stall.

beneath it lies a large crypt with imposingly wide vaults. These are supported by four pillars which, instead of standing on ordinary pedestals, rest on recumbent lions; before the almost completely sculptural pillars are representations of the four evangelists. Their relationship to the portal figures of St. Trophime in Arles is obvious. The pillars once carried a projecting pulpit above the arch of the crypt. This pulpit also served as a baldachin for the Altar of the Cross just beneath it, consecrated in 1208.

Chur cathedral forms a modest link between Western art and history. It exemplifies the Romanesque in the heaviness of its walls, pillars, and figure capitals and progressive Gothic ideas in its spaciousness, its bay articulation of nave and aisles, and its ogival vaults. The art within its walls spans a period of some 1500 years: the presumably late antique altar platform, the Carolingian railings, Romanesque stone sculptures, the gravestone of Ortlieb von Brandis, the Gothic carved altar, the richly turreted tabernacle, the baroque pulpit, the classicist epitaph of Bishop Dionysius von Rost (1793). The same continuity is found in the cathedral treasury, a testimony to the living Christian tradition on the northern face of the Alps.

LAUSANNE

The Cathedral of
Notre Dame

The cathedral of Lausanne seems not so much "enthroned" on the hills of the Old City as resting there. The structure appears to sprawl, but actually it is the buildings of the bishop's see that are clustered behind it.

The original cathedral was the Church of St.-Maire, named after the eminent bishop. The present-day church stands on the site of a late Roman fortress, or castrum. About 800, during the time of Charlemagne, it was partly torn down to accommodate a church in the Lombardian tradition—triple-naved with straight, walled-in apses in a row. A new and larger structure, now with a choir passageway, porch, and baptistery, replaced the first church about 1000. Its successor is the present cathedral, its choir passageway—still Romanesque—begun about 1173 under Bishop Landry de Durnes, and, after a lengthy interruption, completed in an energetic early Gothic style. About 1590, Bishop Marius, after he was forced from his seat at Aventicum, transferred himself to Lausanne.

The unknown architect of this, Switzerland's largest and most impressive Gothic church, was

not a man of extremes. To be sure, the building extends to a length of almost a hundred meters but it contains nothing disquietingly ambitious, no blinding light, and no darkness. Outside as well as inside the church is a well-balanced, harmonious whole. No single detail demands one's attention, yet each element has its own place.

The layout is regular and provides for a triple-naved church with transept, ambulatory, and a double-towered facade on the west. The short, apselike choir is joined to the transept in the Romanesque-Cistercian tradition. The choir and transept form one entity and the lone west tower, another. Between the two stretches the nave. Schooled in Romanesque conventions, the Master of Lausanne must have enjoyed arranging the consistently designed structures in fantastic patterns. For the double chapel in the crossing and the shape of the south tower he used the cathedral at Laon as a model. Not satisfied with the traditional alternation between column and clustered pier as supports for the nave, he flanked his piers with small columns of varying diameters. The bases and plinths are

53

Lausanne cathedral is one of the most beautiful early Gothic churches in the world. It affords many surprising perspectives, such as that into the two-story chapels in the transept. The plain, absolute stone architecture was originally colored and the building furnished with different liturgical appointments.

consciously differentiated in size and form. A six-part ribbed vault makes the traditional alternating of "strong" and "weak" supports logical.

The perspectives at Lausanne are a joy. Before the west front there is the sumptuous, figure-laden Late Gothic portal commissioned by Bishop Aymon de Montfalcon in the early sixteenth century. Previously, the thirteenth-century porch had been open on the west side, yet its inserted ogival arches supported by two-story clustered piers gave it an enclosed sense. Today one can look between the arches to see the subtle oval form of the hall, where the enthroned Virgin Mary sits before the latticelike wall above the inner portal. Console-supported pillars stand before the rounded, apselike wall. Until the end of the fifteenth century, another ground-floor room, open on both sides, adjoined the porch between the towers. Above this large bay lay a great gallery. Today the side wall is closed and the former rather curious arrangement given up. Only the extraordinary depth of the rearmost bays and the unusual form of the pillars are reminders of the old plan.

Nothing in the interior is so striking as the wonderful "Rose of Lausanne," the great round window in the south transept. The master builder even interrupted the series of triforium arches in order to let its light pour, unconfined, into the entire breadth of the nave. In the outer ring is a square; above it diagonally placed squares unfold, petallike, from the middle in half circles and three-quarter circles, freely suspended and yet contained. Thus the Rose of Lausanne is developed entirely from the perfect forms of the circle and the square. Again and again the image of the cross, the sign of redemption, is formed. In their stone frame round glass disks represent the "Delivered World." Around the Redeemer, who has taken all unto him, the story of the Creation is illustrated with images of the months and the signs of the zodiac, symbols of the elements and the four rivers of Paradise. Red, blue, and yellow are the colors of this portrayal of the universe. Its style is strongly influenced by the additive art of the Romanesque, both in overall setting and in figurative style. This most important example of early Gothic stained glass in Switzerland is traditionally attributed to Peter of Arras, a northern Frenchman.

Another work of similar significance in Swiss art is to be found here: the Apostle Portal on the south side of the church, also known as "portail peint" because its figures still possess the remnants of their original colors. In four groups of three, the life-size apostles stand around an open vaulted hall, witnesses to the triumph of Mary. Over the portal, we see her entombed, awakened by angels, and crowned by her divine son; she is a figure of majesty and at the same time indulgent goodwill. Unfortunately the rapid deterioration of the Apostle Portal in recent decades—perhaps a consequence of air pollution—has made protective measures imperative, and photography is now prohibited.

The cathedral is no longer an episcopal see. At the end of 1536 Bernese troops advanced against Lausanne and ended the rule of the bishop. The altars were demolished by official order. From the opulently appointed cathedral a simple parish church was created. Its nave served for religious ceremonies. The choir, however, was separated by a screen that was not removed until the nineteenth century and was used for scientific lectures and official secular acts. But to many Lausanne cathedral has remained, as it did for centuries, a spiritual home and center.

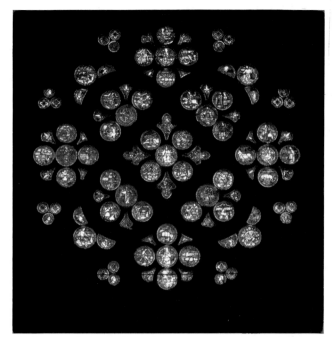

The cross and the circle and square are elements that account for the vividness of the rose window in the south transept of Lausanne cathedral. Its panes depict the universe in images of the Redemption.

ST. GALL

The Cathedral of St. Gall

The Cathedral of St. Gall was not built as a bishop's church. It is more a monument to the blossoming of Benedictine monasticism, which found its expression in the baroque renovation of most of the South German convents.

The abbey, founded as a hermitage in the seventh century by the Irish missionary Gallus, assumed the Benedictine rule under the Abbot Otmar in 749 and was among the most important cultural centers of the Middle Ages. Tuotilo, the Eckhardts, and Notker the German worked here. The Abbot Grimald was chancellor to Louis II of Germany, and the abbey library houses many treasures from this golden era, such as the ivory panels of Tuotilo, the Folchart Psalter, and one of the most important documents of Carolingian architecture, the St. Gall monastery ground plans, drawn in about 830 at the Reichenau abbey for Abbot Gozbart.

Few buildings remain from that great time. Only the crypts at either end of the church, which contain the bones of the founders, Gallus and Otmar, indicate the scale and direction the

cathedral has taken over the centuries. The existing baroque structure was begun in 1755 as one of the last of the great abbey churches and was formally completed in 1767. Its furnishings were still fragmentary when the young canton of St. Gall gave up the princely abbey in 1805 and declared the church its official house of worship. The cloister church of St. Gall reached the rank of bishop's church in 1823, at about the time its earlier rival, the historical Cathedral of Our Blessed Lady in Constance, lost its preeminence.

Plans and designs were submitted beginning in the early eighteenth century. Abbot Coelestin II Gugger von Standach began the construction in 1755 and gave Peter Thumb the exclusive commission for a "seemly navim ecclesiae," for

---

The cathedral of St. Gall was originally built (1755–1767) as a conventual church of the Benedictine order. The east facade, one of the last such works of the baroque period, was built by Johann Michael Beer of Bildstein and Josef Feuchtmayer.

56

the convent resisted dismantling of the fifteenth-century Gothic choir. As the new building advanced, however, it was decided to renovate the east section and give it a grand double-towered facade. That task was entrusted in 1761 to Meister Johann Michael Beer of Bildstein, who was chosen to replace the aging Thumb. Assisting von Bildstein were his nephew, Johann Ferdinand Beer, the cloister brother Gabriel Looser, and the sculptor Josef Anton Feuchtmayer.

One would never think that the cathedral was built in two stages. Between two wings of equal length the main portal leads into a great cupolaed room. The rhythm of the arches to the side cupolas and the alternation of slender and massive pillars rising to the cornices make the St. Gall rotunda one of the most beautiful of all the late baroque. East and west, the depths of the nave and the choir are equally massive, pilastered halls in the Vorarlberg tradition. In this majestic but unemotional repose lies the end of the turbulent baroque and the beginnings of a new classicism.

Though waning, the baroque tensions are nonetheless evident. The pillars jut forward and hide the high windows so that the nave, choir, and rotunda are elegantly separated and at the same time joined. And in the cornices of the octagon a circular movement begins and extends into the side rooms, coming to rest only at the zenith of Heaven, the opening above the arches.

More baroque features are effected by painting, ornamentation, and furnishings. With a view to an integrated interior design, Abbot Coelestin gave the entire St. Gall project to one man: Christian Wenzinger, the widely traveled sculptor and decorative craftsman from Freiburg in Breisgau. He brought proven assistants with him to execute his conception and, in the choir, continue it independently without his collaboration. Josef Wannenmacher painted the ceiling frescoes, and the brothers Johann Georg and Matthias Gigl provided the stucco work. Wenzinger's personal contributions are the figured reliefs in the cupola room. Fidel Sporer, who carved the balusters of the benches, continued the tradition of the master of late baroque sculpture, Josef Anton Feuchtmayer, who completed the confessionals and then did the unique choir benches. The benches represent the final work of his long career and its high point. Two altars are also from his hand; the four others, the pulpit, and the choir screen were done by successors from his workshop.

Wenzinger's unique contribution are the original colors, which give St. Gall its unmistakeable character. The pictures above the white piers are painted in somber, velvety colors in a tempera technique on a red ground and framed by a dark red band trimmed with green stucco. The figure groupings and reliefs are done in warm, ocher tones. All of this is in perfect harmony with the reddish marble altars and the honey-colored woodwork that surrounds the gray, blue, and gold reliefs.

The decoration divides the symmetrical space according to its functions, or suggests such a division. There is a uniform flow from west to east; the ceiling paintings, except for the westernmost, presuppose the eastward gaze of the onlooker. The church pews and the confessionals in the aisles point to the octagon that connects the people's church to that of the monks, for it too flows into the central space. The choir screen, doubly concave, directs the eye to the choir and echoes the circular sweep of the architecture, as do the altars behind it. At the choir, with its organ console, the movement stops. By the pause one is reminded that it is

The center of the cathedral's symmetrical church space is the large rotunda. The color of the brilliant church interior is striking. The decoration is the work of Christian Wenzinger.

here that the canonical hours are chanted.

The high altar and the gallery in the west choir came more than a half century after construction of the new church began. Just as classical traits are hidden in baroque churches, so here, in the classical altar, baroque touches are nestled in the apse. The painting of the Ascension, dated 1644, maintains another of its many links to its rich, meaningful past.

In the choir stalls at St. Gall (finished 1768), Josef Anton Feuchtmayer created one of Europe's masterpieces. Above the rows of seats largescale reliefs of alabaster and gold depict scenes from the life of St. Benedict. A restlessly contoured organ housing completes the effect.

PRAGUE

The Cathedral of St. Vitus

The crown of the "Golden City" of Prague is Hradschin, the Prague Castle. And rising above the fortress is the St. Vitus Cathedral.

The arrangement is a pictorial symbol of a basic theme in Bohemian history: the Bohemian church was beholden to secular powers for ecclesiastical appointments. The first Bohemian saint was also the first Christian duke, Wenceslas. And the second, yet more popular, was John of Nepomuk, vicar general of the archdiocese of Prague. On March 20, 1393, Wenceslas IV, an enemy to virtually everybody, ordered John brutally tortured and thrown half-dead from the Karlsbrucke into the Moldau because he would not reveal the content of the queen's confession.

In the late fourteenth century Prague looked back on a glorious epoch, which would be grandly recorded by Hartmann Schedel in his world history a hundred years later: "At last, in the time of the Emperor Charles IV, the kingdom of Bohemia rose to great power and glory and wondrous station. No other kingdom in all of Europe could equal it. Nowhere could

one find so many marvels, churches so splendid, so vast, ornamented with windows so beautiful, buildings so impressive." Prague owes even its cathedral to Charles IV. With his father, John, the reigning emperor, he laid the cornerstone in 1344 so that the city, elevated to an archdiocese, would have a worthy cathedral—but one within his castle, on the site of St. Wenceslas's grave.

It was to be a Gothic cathedral after the French model that Charles knew as a student in Paris. Accordingly, he commissioned a French architect, Matthias of Arras, who fashioned a high choir after the example of the Cathedral of Narbonne. In choosing a successor to Matthias, Charles IV made a daring and imaginative decision, summoning one Peter Parler, only twenty-three, from Schwäbish Gmünd. Parler, under

---

The cathedral of St. Vitus in Prague, surrounded by the Hradschin Castle but dominating it, expresses architecturally the relationship of secular and spiritual power in Bohemia.

62

Peter Parler, called to Prague to continue the cathedral construction under Emperor Charles IV, installed an upper story almost completely made of glass above the closed ambulatory of Matthias of Arras. Among the portrait busts in its gallery is one of Charles, whose rule signaled a golden age for Prague.

his father, had been occupied with the building of the Heiligkreuzmunster. The young master now had to carry on the irreproachable plans of his predecessors; in fact, part of the building was already completed. Parler decided to give play to his creative fantasy. He contrasted the somber area of the arcades with a higher level inundated with light. A continuous balustrade distinctly divided the two parts. In a more recessed area, he created a graceful screen of window transoms and connected them to the upper part to form a regular rhythm unbroken by the small columns projecting between the windows. In front of these "harps" he placed a slant-roofed, light triforium, which first projects beyond the pillars only to incline back almost to the windows. A gentle forward and backward vacillation emerged—a play between a flat glass wall and restless structure, which at once disregards the bay formation and conforms to it. Quite logically, a net vault stretches muscularly above the choir. The nave was not erected until the nineteenth century. But Peter Parler did plan the mighty bell tower to the west of the crossing which, uncompleted but soaring to a considerable height, bore a baroque cupola and four droll "onions" on its supporting arches. Parler also applied himself to the triforium as sculptor and created the famous portrait gallery which includes his own likeness.

In the Wenceslas Chapel Parler drew on the art of the Middle Ages to create a fittingly Gothic memorial to the saint. On the ironclad gate hangs the ring from the church door in Benzlau, to which Wenceslas clung as his brother rushed forth to stab him in 929. Inside the chapel, we feel as if we are in the dimly lit interior of a reliquary, whose walls are inlaid

Probably the most sacred place in Bohemia is the dark, secretive Wenceslas Chapel, sepulcher of Wenceslas, national patron saint and the first Christian duke of Bohemia. The walls are inlaid with precious gems and covered with frescos, and the sacred furnishings bespeak a timeless piety.

with large semiprecious stones in golden mountings. On the east wall stands a single sculpture, one of Wenceslas—the sole resident, as it were, of his chapel. Painted scenes from his life are hung about the walls. Many storms raged around Prague and the castle; but none has violated the sanctity of this place. One cannot help feeling awe as he leaves the sanctuary.

A more serene triumph over sorrow is seen in the silver tomb which Josef Emanuel Fischer von Erlach created in 1733 for the father confessor John of Nepomuk, who had been canonized four years earlier. Beneath a suspended baldachin in a Gothic vault angels hold up the coffin from which the saint seems to rise to regard the crucifix. His head is crowned by a halo studded with five stars which spell *Tacui:* "*I was silent.*"

After the main structure was finished, foreman Anton Pilgram was able to devote his energies to the religious appointments of the cathedral and build the "organ foot" in the left side nave and the pulpit (1510–1515). His self-portrait appears on both. On the pupit, it's in a false window beneath the stairs, gaining him the eternal nickname "the window-gawker."

The figure in the west end of the church honors vicar general John of Nepomuk. Nepomuk, confessor to the queen, was thrown into the Moldau River by Wenceslas IV because he refused to divulge the nature of her confession. The splendid silver tomb in the ambulatory was the work of Josef Emanuel Fischer von Erlach (1733).

VIENNA

The Cathedral of St. Stephan

One could hardly find a cathedral so perfectly centered in a city as the cathedral of Vienna. The steeple of its tower is the axis of the town; or, in the words of Adalbert Stifter, the church is "a center around which the city gravitates, and the steeple underlines the importance of this majestic edifice" (*Aus dem alten Wien*). The massive, steep roof is like some monumentally rendered hip-roof on a private home. It shelters everything beneath it, and the vivid crenellated modeling of its brick surfaces lend it an exotic charm.

In character the Cathedral of St. Stephan is reminiscent of San Marco in Venice. In both something mysterious prevails. At San Marco it may be the gold and the dim light, but here it is perhaps the space and the richly picturesque baroque decoration—which before the war was even richer—that makes the feet of the piers unnoticeable and complicates one's orientation. It may be the dark heights of the windowless central nave rising over the lateral naves or the marvelously illogical but tasteful baldachins before the pier shafts and their sculpted saints.

Or is it the dissolving network of the vaults, the attenuated light?

The great hall was created in two stages. Beginning in 1304 the choir was built as a hall, each of whose three equally high naves had its own five-sided closing. The nave was completed in 1455 by Hans Puchsbaum, who incorporated the late Romanesque west front of the previous building. The 345 foot (137 meter) high south tower at the end of the transept was completed by Peter and Hans von Prachatitz between 1407 and 1433. From the beginning the church was favored by the dukes of Austria, who deemed it their burial place. At first only a parish church, in 1363 it became the patron church of the collegiate chapter of the castle chapel. The name of St. Stephan is a remnant of the period before

---

The tower of St. Stephan's is the pivotal point and symbol of Vienna. It is not linked to the mighty body of the church but stands, like its never-completed counterpart, along the flank of the building.

The tomb of Emperor Frederick III was begun in 1463 by Niklaus Gerhaert von Leyen, who was summoned from Strassburg for the task. The covering slab with prone figure is probably by his own hand.

The hall church with several "equal" naves is a special development of German Gothic. St. Stephan's is one of the principle examples of this variation.

the church was a cathedral and belonged to the diocese of Passau.

This emperor's tomb stands in the elevated closing of the Apostle Choir on the south side. It is a magnificent catafalque of red and white spotted marble, surrounded by a balustrade. The design is by Niklaus Gerhaert von Leyen, who probably also did the remarkable ceiling paneling after Friedrich called him from Strassburg in 1463. The tomb bears an image of the emperor in full regalia, crowned and holding the dalmatic and pluvial, references to his role as protector of Christianity, the scepter, and the imperial orb. The slab is not treated as a single, homogeneous stone surface upon which the figure lies, but is fissured by dark recesses which, together with the spotted stone as it runs against the sculptural articulation, unite figure and decor in a flickering,impressionistic picture. On the pedestals of the pillars, the electors stand deathwatch. It is not great political deeds that are immortalized here but the spiritual benefactions of the deceased. Still, his secular importance is extolled in the coats of arms and an inscription lists his titles and territorial dominions, among them Kyburg, Schenkenberg, Rapperswil, Raron, Froburg, and Lenzburg. At his feet is the coat of arms of the Hapsburgs.

Going back into the main sanctuary, one's attention is caught by the pulpit. When the building was almost completed, Anton Pilgram, chief of the building corporation from 1510 to 1515, devoted his energies to decoration and the results were the balcony unfolding on a tongued, ribbed console for the display of an organ, and the pulpit, made from a single block of stone. The four Western church fathers gaze out of its balustrade. On a similar scale but in a less prominent place, Pilgram also represented himself. With compasses in hand, he looks out from a window beneath the pulpit steps. Another self-portrait, a bust, serves as a support for the organ. It shows a man in his middle years, with gaunt cheeks and wrinkled skin to which the fleshy lips do not seem suited. Here an artist has consciously left a signatory monument and heralded humanism in art.

SALZBURG

The Cathedral of St. Rupert and St. Vergil

Salzburg cathedral was the first church north of the Alps to consciously and directly correspond to Italian baroque models, especially to one, the Jesuit church Il Gesù in Rome, often considered the cradle of baroque architecture. In Salzburg, instead of a picturesque nave with aisles, a mighty space is unified beneath an encompassing barrel vault. Instead of side naves, intimate chapels are linked to the main room by oratories.

The architect Santino Solari went back to Gesù for the basic form of the Salzburg cathedral, with its octagonal lantern and two-tiered chapels flanking the nave. St. Peter's may have been the model for the rounded transept closings, their assimilation into the main apse, the rich fenestration, and the monumental orchestration of the nave with double pilasters beneath forward and backward-vaulted framework. But more than either of these models, the Salzburg cathedral makes use of light. The nave itself has no openings and receives only scant illumination from the

The energy with which the octagonal dome of Salzburg Cathedral rises toward the sky is emphasized by the decorations of plaster and paint.

The dramatic contrast between the radiant light of the choir and transepts and the semidarkness of the nave underlines the power and dynamics of early baroque architecture. Not only Il Gesù and St. Peter's in Rome but the cathedral of Como were important influences here.

chapels and oratories, which also have few windows. But a flood of light pours into the crossing and choir and streams back up the congregational nave. At Salzburg it can rightly be said that light comes to the people only from the altar.

It was the teaching church of the Counter-Reformation after the Council of Trent. Vigorously molded white stucco is applied to the snow-white walls and ceilings. The stucco is not freely modeled but poured and mounted, and made conspicuous by the use of darkened contours and projecting supports. Pillars and double arches remain almost unadorned, with only their inner surfaces decorated. Colored and figural painting is limited to small, precisely defined areas. Only in the cupola drum is there a striking illusionistic effect.

By comparison with the spotless, elegant interior, the outer walls are utterly plain. Only the west end is adorned, presenting a double-tower *massiv* with a gable-crowned central facade, which contains an open porch. The cathedral was also to be the chief model for baroque variations on the twin-towered church front favored in southern Germany since the eleventh century.

Salzburg was always a residence for great men. The prince-archbishops of Salzburg assumed the title of primate of all Germany and held brilliant courts, especially during the baroque period. Thus the city has an emphatically Italianate face and has itself become a baroque work in which the cathedral is imbedded.

In Salzburg Cathedral, Roman baroque gained a foothold north of the Alps. It commands a courtyard enclosed by arches and palace buildings.

The cathedral's forerunner of the twelfth century was, with its five naves, the largest homogeneous Romanesque church outside Italy. A catastrophic fire destroyed it in 1598, and, after several projects were considered and stalemated, the new building was begun according to Solari's plans in 1614. It was essentially completed in 1618.

There is one piece that should be mentioned, the great Romanesque bronze baptismal font, cast in 1311. It rests on four supine lions of the twelfth century and displays on its underside, beneath arch formations, a gallery of saintly bishops.

Sparseness of furnishings in medieval churches is generally attributed to iconoclasms, catastrophes, renovations, or "purifications" of style, but the bareness of Salzburg is intentional. The ancillary altars are banished to the chapels and side rooms, but in the central church space everything is directed toward the high altar in the apse. It is like a stage bathed in floodlight. The art of such dramatic focus was to be developed to its fullest in the Jesuit churches.

CONSTANCE

The Cathedral of Our Blessed Lady

The Cathedral of Our Blessed Lady in Constance is not often included in books on famous churches or cathedrals. Yet it is one of the most precious monuments of Central Europe and one of the most venerated German churches.

Its greatness lies in its amalgam of styles of all periods from the tenth century onward. The history of the cathedral is plainly visible to anyone who knows how to "read" architecture.

The overall form is evident in the ground plan: a triple-naved basilica with transept, flat-closed choir with crypts and annexes, the whole imbedded in a complex of buildings to the north and the east. On the west side rises a robust escarpment of masonry—the towers.

The plan was conceived under Bishop Rumold in 1054. He commissioned the naves separated by mighty sandstone piers with carved shafts five meters high. Parts of the choir area, including the hall crypts, subdivided by six pillars, are salvaged from the Ottonian cathedral, which collapsed in 1052. Originally the church was furnished with painted wooden ceilings, similar to but more compact than the Schaffhauser cathedral, consecrated in 1103.

The Council of Constance (1414–1418) accounts indirectly for the Gothic style of the church. King Sigmund convened the council to restore unity to the church, which was plagued with heresies and floundering under three antipopes. Besides the putative pope, the gathering included 3 patriarchs, 23 cardinals, 93 archbishops, 151 bishops, 100 abbots, 50 priors, and, as the highest representatives of secular power, the king and queen and their nobles. Also attending were spokesmen for science and throngs of merchants and craftsmen. Many artists were also present, providing a great stimulus to artistic activity in the Bodensee city. John XXIII, who seemed to be the only anti-pope present, was immediately deposed, and Martin V was named the new pope. One tragic element encroached on this restitution of unity: Czech reformer Jan Hus, who had come to Constance to defend the teachings of Wycklif, was condemned by the council and burned at the stake.

One of the most elegant early Gothic artifacts on the Bodensee is the Holy Tomb in the Maurice Rotunda, a goal of pilgrims who could not go to Jerusalem.

The cultural renaissance brought to the city by the council would have ebbed had it not been for Bishop Otto III of Hachberg, a great patron of art, who lived in the Constance Pfalz.

During the Gothic period the great windows in the choir and crossing, the ribbed vaults, the lateral naves, and the flanking row of chapels were built. These were all furnished in the changing styles of subsequent periods. The most singular "Gothicized" element in the cathedral is the spiral staircase in the north transept by Master Antoni, who was lodge chief and chaplain of the Ottilia Altar. Antoni was influenced by the French, and the nearest prototype of the Constance staircase was in the erstwhile castle of Bourges. The original plan at Constance called for upstairs rooms; happily the staircase remains even though the plan was abandoned. Antoni built the stair like a sacred vessel: it followed the church wall until it reached the actual spiral. Above that a substantial "foot" supports the six-sided casing. In the lowest tier of the casing are bas-relief scenes from the life of the Virgin: the fall of Gideon and the Annunciation, the Nativity, and the Burning Bush. The works at the top of the cage correspond to relief panels and are linked through rungs introduced into the middle of each panel. At the edges are groups of two apostles, pediments, and arches carved from a single block of stone. We marvel at the coherence of the individual proportions and the general harmony of the whole.

The cathedral of Constance is at heart a Romanesque basilica, and with its outlying buildings and art treasures from many centuries is an image and memory of the grandeur of the past. Its galleries and organ front are rare examples of the transitional style between Late Gothic and Renaissance.

In the late Gothic carved choir stalls of Simon Haider and Heinrich Iselins (1466–1471) we can read the development of the Gothic style over the thirty years since the building of the staircase.

Today one's gaze goes unhindered to the early classical (1775–1776) high altar of Michel d'Ixnard, who was assigned the decoration of the choir. That area is one of the youngest parts of the concert of styles and periods that meet at Constance.

At the west end of the church the organ with its magnificent front and ornamented console arrests our attention. In it late Gothic and progressive Renaissance elements unite in a willful mixture. A flattened arch transversing the west wall bears voluted consoles with pierced extremities. In the middle a bearded man's face appears, probably a self-portrait of the master builder, Lorenz Reder. Above the small clustered piers, which emerge from the consoles and abruptly terminate, are Late Gothic traceried balconies. In the hollows of the arches cherubs cavort without regard for Gothic dignity. Between Gothic baldachins ornamental grotesqueries of about 1515 protrude.

The organ, by Master Hans Schentzer of Stuttgart, was the largest in Germany. In 1618 Michael Praetorius wrote, "The organ of Constance must be an extremely large instrument. Has more than 3000 pipes and 70 registers." Unfortunately nothing is left of the great instrument.

What remains, however, is the magnificent front, executed in 1518, with its pillars garlanded by lush foliage, the golden adornment on a red ground, and the painting of Matthaus Gutrecht, who also embellished the great doors to the console. Originally it was even more grand than it is today, for in 1680 the pedal turrets had to be reduced to allow installation of the Gothic vaulting.

In making a circuit of the church, one's eyes turn to the latticed closings of the side chapels. In them a history of the ironmonger's craft can be read. In the Chapel of the Virgin one's attention is drawn to the magnificent baroque marble altar, and the Romanesque copper plates, with golden representations of Christ and the two diocesan patrons, Konrad and Pelagius, are almost overlooked. Until 1924 they shone from the heights of the choir gable, but they now look somewhat out of place above the south portal.

The cathedral of Constance, then, does not have the bright, easy countenance of a young person; its beauty has many layers, is more subtle and mysterious. It is the beauty of traces left by the centuries.

SPEYER

The Cathedral of St. Mary

Too often we hear that art must not imitate the past, so the masters seem to have brilliantly pushed on to renovate, complete or add to the work of earlier periods in their own styles. The imperial cathedral at Speyer is evidence of just the opposite principle—a monument to reconstruction of the past.

This church building, chosen by German kings and Roman emperors for their own interment, has not reached us undamaged. It survived centuries and several fires rather well until, on Pentecost Day, 1689, the conquering troops of the Sun King put the city to the torch. The fire reached the cathedral and the possessions of the citizens who had taken refuge there. The western nave vaulting succumbed to the ovenlike heat, and for almost ten years the cathedral lay in ruins. Then the intact east part of the nave was newly roofed and the ruined western half demolished.

Today the cathedral stands as it once existed. Franz Ignaz Neumann, son of the famed Balthasar, builder of Vierzehnheiligen and Neresheim, rebuilt the destroyed parts in 1772–1778 in the Roman style which then was popular. In the nineteenth century the job was finished with the reconstruction of the western transept, which had been leveled for safety reasons in 1854. The rest of the cathedral barely escaped demolition, the fate of its great rival, the cloister church of Cluny, under Napoleon.

King Ludwig I of Bavaria showed his admiration for medieval German painting by commissioning Johann Schraudolph to paint the interior of Speyer cathedral in 1846–1853. After the restorations of our own century, little remains of Schraudolph's work, except in the spaces above the arcades of the central nave.

Almost everyone who passes through the portals of Speyer is struck by the purity of the architecture. Here one finds only natural stone and white plaster. No ornamentation or furnishings intrude. In the clear light, darkening toward the apse, the impression is one of singular grandeur.

The central nave is independent of the side aisles. In fact three long parallel rooms open into the crossing, though the impression is one of a three-naved room subdivided by pillars. While all the piers in the lateral naves are identical, toward the central nave every other one is strengthened by a pilaster and sturdy, semicircular projections which show, halfway up, peculiar "capitals." These serve as supports for the middle nave vaulting. If one imagines these reinforcements removed, he will see a uniform wall broken at regular intervals by false arcades. In fact this very condition once existed; the cathedral acquired its final form in two stages.

The cornerstone of the first building was laid in 1030 by Salier Konrad II, crowned emperor in Rome in 1027. The church comprised a pillared basilica with a two-storied western transept and three naves, of which those on the side were vaulted and the middle one, with transept and crossing, was flat-ceilinged. There were also two pairs of towers, one pair to the side of the choir, the other at the east end, and probably a dominating central tower.

In 1080 Henry IV, the penitent of Canossa, had the whole building vaulted—a brilliant feat for that time—and ordered the crossing and apse rebuilt. The outside walls were wainscoted with square stones and, as the vaulting required greater height, a dwarf-arched gallery was introduced. This structure, completed in 1106, survived the baroque restorers and exists today.

The charming alternation of red-yellow stone and white surfaces does not conform, to be sure, to the original style of the cathedral. Red was the color of the ancient emperors, and in the course of restorations workers discovered fragments of the red decoration that probably covered the entire interior.

The strength of the walls is awesome. The west wall is six meters thick, and the walls of the crossing afford space for small recessed chapels.

Also surprising in the crossing is the appearance of Corinthian capitals, handsomely worked and scrupulously close to ancient models, and of pillars of a type found nowhere else in the upper church. The walls are pierced with richly *étagé* windows. Details such as these link the building inextricably with the time of Henry IV. But the original structure, from 1030, did not reflect its High Romanesque origins so clearly; for all its monumentality it presented certain "delicate" traits. These traits remain today in the sickle-shaped double arches of the vault, which are free of the strict concentric quality that marks the art of the twelfth century. The Romanesque flourished along the Rhine even as the first Gothic churches were going up in France.

Another part of the original building is the monumental crypt beneath the crossing and choir, where the cathedral founders, Konrad II and Gisela, repose. The crypt was chosen as a tomb site by many kings and emperors. Rudolf of Hapsburg, a prominent figure in Swiss history who died in 1291, is also buried here. His tombstone (about 1500) stands at the entrance to the imperial tomb and depicts the king in an ankle-length gown with billowing folds, his feet supported by a small lion, a crown on his head and the imperial orb in the left hand.

The crypt itself is a large subchurch, comprising four square rooms corresponding to the choir, the crossing, and the transept arms of the upper cathedral and separated by pillars into

As rich in towers as a fortress, with transept, central tower, and west front, the cathedral sits enthroned on its hill above the Rhine. Founded in 1030 by Emperor Konrad II, it was rebuilt in its present form by Henry IV (1080–1106).

82

At Speyer, the spacious hall crypt beneath the crossing, transepts, and choir is the burial place of many emperors and kings. In the background, the tombstone of King Rudolf of Hapsburg (about 1300).

The view into the north transept shows the powerful beauty of the architecture. The large windows effectively break up the surface of the wall, thick enough to house small chapels.

nine square bays. The pillars are a graceful compromise between compactness and elegance. They stand on graduated pedestals with steep bases of two tori with flat chamfers between them. Their unadorned cubelike capitals carry a profiled cover plate to dispatch the double arches and the edges of the vaulting. Such hall crypts evolved from the narrow catacombs beneath early medieval churches, which were modified during Carolingian times as the first hall-type structures (St. Gall, Reichenau), and finally became veritable subchurches with whole forests of columns.

Speyer cathedral leaves its final impression—one of a natural, comfortable grandeur without a trace of ostentation, an imperial ambience.

COLOGNE

The Cathedral of St. Peter

It seemed the fate of the Cathedral Church of St. Peter in Cologne to remain incomplete. In the sixteenth century construction was halted after work on the choir was temporarily terminated. For a whole century the silent, motionless crane on the massive stump of the south tower was one of the distinctive features of the city. Then, in the nineteenth century, the art of the Middle Ages was reincarnated in romanticism. Rediscovery of the original plans for the west facade gave the undertaking a powerful impetus. After four hundred years, the cathedral corporation became active again.

In Cologne it was Sulpiz Boisserée who championed the completion of the cathedral. He arranged for resumption of the construction and convinced many eminent personages to join the cause—among them Goethe, Görres, Georg Forster, Friedrich Schlegel, and the crown prince, later king of Prussia, Friedrich Wilhelm III. Boisserée exhorted them to "completion of the cathedral as thanks to God for the liberation of the fatherland from French bondage." The motivation was admittedly less religious than nationalistic. It is ironical that the finished church had its artistic sources in France.

Before completion of the fragmentary parts—crossing, nave, and towers—could be considered, it was necessary to reinforce the existing structure, namely the gigantic choir. In 1821 the venerable old archdiocese of Cologne was reinstituted by a papal bull. The cathedral's wide halls had been utterly profaned during the French period and misused as a hayloft and military prison. In 1841 a cathedral builders' union was founded. The Prussian state did its part, and collections and a "cathedral tax" brought in more revenue. On September 4, 1842, the king laid the new "cornerstone" for the continued building, and a force of four hundred workers started the task.

In 1848 the main nave was covered by a temporary roof, and one of the first celebrations in the rehabilitated cathedral was the six hundredth anniversary of the laying of the original cornerstone. In 1863, after the vaulting had been completed, the "temporary" partition wall between choir and nave was removed and for the first time the interior space could be seen as a whole. From then on attention was directed to the towers, which received their crowning crosses in 1880.

Emperor Wilhelm I was present at the celebration of completion, but the archbishop of Cologne, during these times of struggle between church and state, lived in exile. The completion ceremony was, like the resumption of the building, more a political than a religious event.

If the Cologne cathedral became a symbol of German political unity in the late nineteenth century, it stood as a battered symbol of hope to a defeated people after World War II. By 1956 it was once again in full use. Let us hope that the polluted air of our own times does not destroy it again.

In 1164 Emperor Friedrich Barbarossa conquered the city of Milan. Reinald von Dassel, his chancellor and the archbishop of Cologne, demanded the relics of the Three Kings and of the Roman legionnaires Felix and Nabor as a reward for his services. He transported the valuable cargo from Milan to Cologne and initiated a golden age for his cathedral church. This was the era of pilgrimages to the Holy Land, and Cologne became a popular detour for the faithful, who paused to pay homage to the Three Kings.

The original cathedral was planned in the Carolingian period and was similar to the plans for the St. Gallen monastery. It must have had an archaic look amidst the masterpieces of the Late Romanesque period, which was just in full flower in the Rhenish countries. In 1247, in accord with the instructions of Archbishop Engelbert the Holy but twenty-two years after his assassination, the chapter initiated work on a new sanctuary.

Even before the idea of renovating the church took form, the relics of the Three Kings had received a luxurious shelter: a miniature church with a towering middle nave and side naves with lean-to roofs, surrounded by arcades on double pillars. In the lower part of the shrine rest the relics of the Magi, in the upper those of Felix and Nabor.

The Shrine of the Three Kings is probably the most famous piece of goldwork of the Middle Ages. Surprisingly, the Three Kings do not appear as principal figures in the decoration of the shrine. They are represented only once—on the front, where they are shown bearing their gifts to the Child Jesus. Behind them stands the German usurper Otto IV (reigned 1198–1215), evidently the donor of the gold-chased reliquary. The baptism of Christ also appears on the front, and in the gable of the shrine we see the Savior as judge. The scenes suggest that the Adoration of the Magi is a metaphor of the glory and victory of Christ. Apostles and prophets appear as witnesses to the glory on the sides of the shrine. On the back surface the scourging of Jesus and the Resurrection are shown.

While the shrine's "architecture," with its round and trefoil arches and cubed capitals, still follows Romanesque conventions, the figures imitate the early Gothic sculpture of France, such as the Virgin Mary carvings on the north portal at Chartres. There are, for example, the same finely wrought folds in the sculpted robes. The most sublime craftsmanship is seen in the seated figures of the prophets and apostles on the long sides of the shrine. The Three Kings Shrine

It is thanks to the romantic revival of the 19th century that the largest cathedral in Germany was finished. Only the medieval choir, begun in 1247, had been completed previously.

The crucifix that Archbishop Gero of Cologne had carved
(969–976). It's the first monumental sculpture of the
Crucifixion in the West.

is the common work of several masters, one of
whom was probably Nikolaus of Verdun,
creator of the shrine to Mary at Tournai and of
the Klosterneuburger Altar. Today the shrine
stands on an elevation behind the high altar of
the cathedral in the conventional mode of
display of the Middle Ages. However, the shrine
originally stood in the apse.

Another singular work of art is at least two
hundred years older: the life-size crucifix of the
Archbishop Gero (969–976), probably the oldest extant monumental cross from the Middle
Ages. It once stood in the middle of the old
cathedral over Gero's tomb. This is the first
known example of the crucified Christ realis-
tically represented as dead: the body is limply
collapsed; the head falls forward; the face is a
mask of suffering, and the eyes are closed. The
presentation, of Carolingian origin, is close to
life, natural and moving. At the head of Jesus is
a receptacle for depositing the Host, which in
the Middle Ages was considered a relic of
Christ. In this regard, the Gero cross was not only an art object but in a very direct sense a
representation of the Savior.

It seems as if, after the Three Kings had
received their shrine of gold and enamel, it was
decided to renovate the cathedral in kind. One
Gerhard, called "master, leader, and stonemason of the Cologne Corporation," apparently
received his training in Amiens and Beauvais.
The latter church inspired his ground plan with
its seven choir chapels or apses and the glazed
windows of the triforium, the passageway over
the side-nave arcades. Going beyond his model,
Gerhard provided for a five- sectioned nave. The
weighty twin-towered facade was planned after
the fourteenth century. Cologne cathedral, then,
is basically a magnification of French cathedral

90

Gothic, with the lush ornamentation of its buttressing providing it with a typically picturesque German style. The flying buttresses disappear in a forest of columns with exuberant pinnacle decoration.

On the inside clustered piers allow the vertical shafts to shoot up without interruption to the shoulders of the vaulting. The crossing, nave, and towers were not built until the nineteenth century, yet it is the medieval choir that remains most important. Among its astonishingly rich decorations are the fourteenth-century paintings on the screen, the Gothic choir stalls, the many tombs of the Cologne archbishops, the magnificent high altar with its ornamental figures, and the wonderful polychrome statues on the pillars.

Finally there is Stephan Lochner's *Dombild*, a triptych painted about 1445 for the municipal chapel and saved by Friedrich Schlegel from destruction during the cathedral profanation. The visit of the Three Kings in Bethlehem is again the central theme. With the Magi are St. Ursula and St. Gereon of Cologne and their companions, a glittering audience of studied opulence, on the wing panels. The fabrics of the robes are affectionately reproduced; the plants and other flora are shown in the most minute detail, and the majesty of the Virgin is gracefully evoked. On the more tranquil outer sides of the leaves, the angel surprises Mary at prayer in her chamber and hails her as Full of Grace. Lochner ingeniously made both leaves seem one space by using uniform perspective from floor to ceiling by means of a continuous, sumptuous curtain backdrop. The garments and furniture that do not strictly follow the laws of centralized perspective still create an illusion of depth, without reducing the decorative flatness of the whole.

The Shrine of the Three Kings, one of the jewels of the goldsmith's art along the Rhine and the Maas of the twelfth and thirteenth centuries. It is probably the most famous German reliquary of the Middle Ages.

TOURNAI

The Cathedral of Notre Dame

Tournai, on the Roman route from Cologne to Boulogne, was Christianized by St. Piat at the end of the third century. Since the early sixth century, the bishop of Tournai has also had the status and functions of a royal count. Even from a distance, the five towers of the bishop's church on the Schelde stand out like a crown. The bundle of towers is a unique monument of Late Romanesque architecture and by itself would suffice to establish the fame of the cathedral.

Created between 1130 and 1213, the towers do not mark the west end of the church but crown the crossing, from which radiate the nave to the west and, like a trefoil to north, east, and south, three equal choirs, after the model of the Rhenish Romanesque. The eastern tower, a High Gothic lantern, did not appear until the thirteenth century. The major rebuilding in the twelfth century was actually a result of the plague, which overran the populace in 1089. Reports of miraculous cures by those who prayed before the statue of the Virgin carried far and wide, and made Tournai, with its "Madonna of the Ailing," a place of pilgrimage.

The feast day of the saint on September 14 culminates in a great procession, in which her venerated image and the reliquaries from the church treasury are borne through the city. In the late Middle Ages the cathedral was often the scene of a colorful spectacle. Forty-two canons belonged to the cathedral chapter. A collegium of twelve grand vicars saw to the ceremonies, supported by more than fifty assisting chaplains. A famous choral school developed and gave us the oldest complete three-part mass, known as "The Mass of Tournai" (about 1330). The religious offices continued throughout the day, from Matins to Compline.

Miracle plays developed particularly well at such pilgrimage places and were presented in the cathedral. At Pentecost, when "Come Holy

---

Flemish tapestries were widely exported as early as the Middle Ages. This example, ordered in 1402 by Toussaint Pryer to decorate the choir at Tournai, relates the life of the city's patron saint, Piat.

92

The cluster of five towers dominates the royal Merovingian city of Tournai like a crown. At the site of the east apse of the original three-tiered building, a lofty, elongated Gothic choir was built.

With the addition of the Gothic choir lantern the outer apses of the original trefoiled sanctuary became a transept. Although the basic structural principles of the nave are respected, the vertical momentum and severe modeling proclaim a Gothic sense of space.

Ghost" was sung, a pigeon was released—a custom still observed in certain monasteries—and pieces of bread, called "Nieulles," were distributed to symbolize the gift of the Holy Spirit. On Easter three deacons advanced to the eastern end of the church to symbolize the three Marys approaching the sepulcher, and a lantern procession of two singing groups was held on Good Friday. On Holy Innocents, the "Bishop of Fools" was elected. This ceremony was far from a sober rite, and yet it demonstrated the close bond between religious and secular life in the Middle Ages and the place of the bizarre in the sacred.

The triple nave results in an unusual wall construction. Three levels of arches are superimposed much like a Roman viaduct but without continuous vertical members, being thus subdivided into fixed bays. This form was characteristic of church construction in Great Britain and found its way into the Gothic mode. The Anglo-Norman influence is also identifiable in the column-rich passageway before the clerestory windows.

Not surprisingly, with the emphasis on horizontal articulation, the role of vaulting was diminished, and the middle nave was given a flat wooden ceiling so that it resembles a banquet room. By contrast, the transept, built on another level, was given vaulting. In comparing it with the nave, it becomes clear that the height of the ground floor and the vertical tendency increased. The vaulting is cautiously close to the ogive; though still within the gravity of the Romanesque, it heralds the new feeling which will find its realization in the Gothic.

In the nave the heights of the galleries correspond to the size of the aisles; in the transept the galleries are similar to a corridor, and the small columns beneath the windows seem merely enhancement for the windows. Finally, the choir is a throwback to the three-story solution of the High Gothic at Amiens, with arcade, triforium, and clerestory.

Only a few works of art in the church survived the Reformation, Revolution, and wars. Among these is the tapestry of St. Piat, donated in 1402 by Canon Toussaint Pryer, chaplain to Philip the Good of Burgundy. The custom of decorating church walls with tapestries is an old one that continued up to baroque times. Rubens produced tapestries for the cathedral at Cologne, and others were exported from Flanders to Spain. The tapestry of St. Piat, 71 feet (22 meters) long and 6½ feet (2 meters) high, was woven by Pierrot Fere of Arras. Scenes from the lives of the converts of Tournai and of St. Eleutherius, bishop during the time of the Franks, unroll in resplendent colors.

The Shrine of the Virgin is the most precious metal piece in the treasury, and it was the privilege of the Ghent citizens to carry it in processions. It is the second surviving signed work of Nikolaus of Verdun and is considered a work of his mature years. It has—like the closely related Shrine of the Three Kings in Cologne—enameled panels and figures in relief. In it the art of the twelfth-century goldsmith reached its epitome and advanced from Romanesque mass to Gothic articulation.

The wall of the Romanesque nave is like a Roman viaduct of superposed arcades. Behind the baroque choir screen glitters the glass backdrop of the Gothic choir.

ANTWERP

The Cathedral of Unserer Lieben Frau

As a major work of Flemish Late Gothic, the cathedral in Antwerp is an example of altered spatial feeling developed from the standard ground plan. The Church of Our Blessed Lady entered history in 1124 when it became headquarters for the canonical chapter of the St. Michael's Church. The space was not adequate to the needs of the large clerical community, and in the thirteenth century the choir was enlarged.

Financing for a new building was acquired in the feast year 1350, and in 1352 plans were drawn up. In 1384–1385 the altars in the choir were built, and the choir vaulting was completed in 1411. After 1422 work was concentrated on the west facade; the single north tower was finished in 1521. Construction after 1430 is documented in the church account books. Although it was decided, one year after completion of the tower, to enlarge the choir, the undertaking did not go far beyond the foundation walls. In 1554 the church was declared a cathedral.

The mighty building resembles the Cologne cathedral in plan: five naves, an ambulatory with radial chapels, and dominant twin towers in the west. But the proportions are different. The bays in the central nave approach a square form; those of the lateral naves are rectangular. Everything seems to be lengthened and aligned uniformly. Two more side naves were added even as the central space was being built. The building finally had seven naves and acquired an almost Spanish breadth.

One of the two west towers was executed in the style of the tower at Strasbourg cathedral but was steeper with a different silhouette. The tower shafts stand free above the eaves of the central nave. The southern tower goes up yet another level before terminating. Its mate,

The cathedral of Antwerp is modeled on those of France. But in the latter stages of its building (after 1350), the language of its form became spare, the elements piled on one another like cubes, and buttressing was discarded. The north tower, visible from afar to sailors, rises like a sculpture to untold heights.

98

Antwerp's most famous son, the brilliant painter Peter Paul Rubens, left the cathedral three great altar paintings. Shown here is a picture normally visible only from afar, the high altar panel of the Assumption of the Virgin (1626).

however, shoots up ever higher, braced on each side by three flying buttresses, which correspond to the double lateral naves. The octagonal tower seems to turn on its own axis, for the octagon does not emanate from copings at the corners of the basic square. Rather, the center pillars of the walls are taken as coordinates and extended so that all wall-like parallels are avoided. Instead there are thin, stringlike masonry formations spanning the corner pillars. Above the platform balconies recapitulate the double motifs of the tower base. The octagon is reduced to a slender diagonal lantern with four supports and culminates in an octagonal spire with double basket, a beacon for the seafarers who put into this rich Hanseatic port.

Here at Antwerp, the mysticism is removed from Gothic. The effect of the church interior is one of strictness, particularly since it lacks the baroque ornamentation that warms the cool atmosphere in other Antwerp churches. The shafts of the piers are nothing more than low profiles, as if made by a comb. They pass without transition into the arches and ribs. The compactness and uniformity of the walls is underlined by flat tracery that abuts the level, fan-shaped balconies beneath the wide windows. Only a corridor reminds us of the triforium of the early Gothic. In the nave and choir crossribbed, bay-accentuating vaults still dominate. In the transept, the vaulting is a netlike, continuously ribbed configuration.

Outside the nave goes without buttressing, but the choir does not. The central nave climbs cleanly above the oblique hip-roofs of the lateral naves.

Peter Paul Rubens (1577–1640), the "painter of princes," was Antwerp's greatest artist. He trained in Italy, and in him, and the powerful workshop he created, the Dutch tradition and

100

Only a close look reveals the cathedral confessionals behind the file of saints
sculpted by Frans Verbruggen, at the beginning of the eighteenth century.

the art of Michelangelo, Tintoretto, Titian, and Caravaggio find their most perfect synthesis. Rubens's esthetic personality profoundly affected the Flemish painting of his time. The paintings on the three main altars in the cathedral are from his hand: the triptych of the Crucifixion (1610), the Descent from the Cross (1612) in the transept, and the high-altar panel of the Assumption of the Virgin Mary (1626). The Virgin is borne upward, followed by the yearning gaze of John, while the women hold the pall and the apostles study the empty sarcophagus in wonder. The focus of the composition is John at the left of the picture. He alone maintains a contact with the light-suffused Virgin.

The art on the pulpit in the nave has an almost national character. About 1820 a baroque pulpit, bearing allegories of the continents with steps and a sound-canopy, was built. Naturalistic branches and interwoven twigwork serve as supports and banisters in which carved birds and other small creatures have settled. Such sculpted "nature pulpits," comparable to the palm pillars in the Chinese Pavilion of Sansouci near Potsdam, were much loved in Flanders throughout the eighteenth century, thanks largely to the activity of the sculptor Michiel von der Voort. The Antwerp pulpit is a late representative of the style.

In the Chapel of Our Blessed Lady, Frans Verbruggen (1660–1724) attached several confessionals to the roomy exterior side nave on the north. He cleverly concealed the separations between the priest's and penitent's seats with life-size figures.

Otherwise, few of the original furnishings of the cathedral have survived. Still extant are the sober central church space with its almost profane naves, the fiery art of Rubens, and, outside, the graceful steeple that is the landmark of Antwerp.

Fantastic creatures are ensconced in the sculpted foliage of the pulpit entranceway. Such "nature pulpits" were a Flemish specialty in the eighteenth century.

SANTIAGO DE COMPOSTELA

The Cathedral of St. James of Compostela

One must go as a pilgrim to Santiago to capture the true sense and force of this extraordinary place, as prominent as Jerusalem and Rome. To reach St. James of Compostela one must climb the Pyrenees to Astorga and press on along seemingly endless winding roads. Gradually the stark terrain gives way to green and gentle hills, and finally the pilgrim sees his destination—Santiago de Compostela.

The apostle James the Older traveled widely before he settled here. He was the promulgator of Christianity in Romanesque Spain and was recalled to the Apostolic Council at Jerusalem in A.D. 44. There he suffered a martyr's death, and his pupils Athanasius and Theodor brought his holy body back to Spain by sea. It is said that two wild bulls pulled the wagon bearing his body from the coast into the green, hilly country of Compostela. A marble tomb was erected to him, but it was all but forgotten in the chaos of subsequent centuries. In 813 the Pelago eremites rediscovered the holy place and it has remained popular with pilgrims until the present.

Excavations show that the Carolingian church of the ninth century was built around a Roman cemetery. That church apparently was succeeded by a larger one, built under King Alfons III of Leon and consecrated in 896. After the Moorish General Almanzor had taken city and church in 997 and had forced his Christian

---

The sumptuous baroque facade of St. James of Compostela built by Fernando Casas y Novoa between 1738 and 1750 not only fronts the wide plaza around the cathedral but dominates the city of Santiago.

104

Behind this spledid facade is a rigorously austere galleried basilica of the eleventh century.

prisoners to carry the plundered bells and towers to Cordova, the old church was rebuilt. A century later, in 1075, Master Bernhard the Old with fifty stonemasons began the grand structure of today. The work was continued by Master Esteban, who finished the present structure in about 1128.

The ground plan looks like a precious Romanesque cross whose four arms are edged with jewels. Lateral naves encircle the long nave and crossing and even flow around the choir as a passage, from which five chapels radiate. Above the side naves lie galleries which open in double arches into the main room. Their vaults support the strong sideward thrust of the high, windowless central nave. Only through the windows of the side naves and galleries, which may once have served as lodgings, does a subdued light invade the central space.

An outside staircase above the wide piazza leads the pilgrim to the high-towered baroque facade, which resembles a rock mass with its exuberant ornamentation (Fernando Casas y Novoa, 1738–1750). Then, through the metal-fitted gates, the visitor glimpses the "Portico de la Gloria," the splendid Romanesque portal of the cathedral. On the middle jamb is a seated statue of St. James holding his pilgrim staff.

Gold gleams in the darkness of the sanctuary. St. James is enthroned above the high altar beneath a golden coffered covering. Pilgrims pass continually through the small gates and clamber up the narrow stairs behind the altar to embrace the apostle of silvered and bejeweled stone. The sculpture was made before 1150 by Master Matteo, who also did the main portal. St. James' relics lie in the crypt beneath the altar, exactly where they were first discovered.

Overhead one hears the endless drone of pilgrims singing mass. In the crossing is the *botafumeiro*, the largest incense dispenser in the world, which swings ponderously during solemn masses. Here the Middle Ages are still alive with all their piety, penitence, joy, primitive roots, perfect form. As a pilgrim guidebook of the twelfth century said of St. James of Compostela: "You find neither error nor irregularity. He who proceeds slowly into the temple will return from there happy and consoled by its wonderful beauty."

Santiago is not only a cathedral but also a holy city. Over the centuries small sanctuaries and chapels, cloisters and sacristies have flourished here. From the outside, therefore, it is difficult to discern the clear, basic Romanesque outline of the cathedral, which is actually similar to other great pilgrim churches, especially to St. Sernin in Toulouse.

Santiago's three towers are a monumental legacy of the baroque. Just as the grand west front and its twin towers dominate the main plaza, so the mighty bell tower dwarfs the intimate Plaza de las Platerias before the south front of the transept. This front is the single remaining Romanesque facade of the cathedral. Its sculptures are among the first of the Spanish Gothic. Everywhere one encounters the pilgrim symbol of St. James, the seashell. It is chiseled into house walls, adorns fountains and statues, and is sold from stalls in all sizes and materials.

Large and small guidebooks are for sale in every language. They have a long ancestry; as early as the twelfth century a French pilgrim wrote the *Liber Sancti Jacobi Apostoli*, two copies of which survive at Compostela and Ripoll. In the third chapter the author gives an exact description of the cathedral and of other sights of the city.

The atmosphere of Santiago seems the same today. And one still marvels at the works of art

The Portico de la Gloria is one of the greatest Romanesque sculptural works in the world. On the middle post, "Santiago"—St. James—appears at the feet of the Divine Judge, who is flanked by the apostles.

of the city and at the consummate architecture of the cathedral. The modern visitor can learn of the same holy routes, sights, and relics that the first pilgrims knew.

Not only pilgrims but many art lovers must have visited Santiago. Shelter, food, and other necessities had to be provided for the pilgrims converging on the city. The Knighthood of St. James, founded during the Crusades, as well as various monasteries boarded the faithful.

Isabella of Castile and Ferdinand of Aragon, the "Catholic monarchs," founded a lodging facility in Santiago as a holy tribute to the apostle. The large blocklike building stands at the north end of the main plaza; its richly ornamented entrance portal gives onto four inner courtyards. The building, refurbished in 1954, is operated today as a hotel.

And the pilgrims still arrive, as they have for so many centuries.

The stone figure of the patron of pilgrims awaits visitors within the baroque sanctuary of his altar.

SEVILLE

The Cathedral of Santa Maria de la Sede

In some European skylines church buildings stand out oddly amidst the motley jumble of houses. In Seville it is different. Here one traipses up the crooked, whitewashed alleyways to the gray brown stone bulk of the cathedral. Despite the enormity of the building, its shape is at first difficult to discern. Only a single dominating feature stands out: its great tower, the "Giralda," whose outside walls are covered with Moorish ornamentation up to the belfry openings.

Seville, known to the Romans as Romula Augusta, derives from the Arabic name "Isbiliah." Christianity took root here in late antiquity and produced in Archbishop Isidor of Seville (560–636) one of the great teaching minds of the Middle Ages. But southern Spain was under Moorish-Arabic rule from 711 until King Ferdinand, the Holy of Castile, reconquered the city in 1248.

The Giralda dates to the last century of Arabian rule, in which Seville was the capital city of a Moorish kingdom. It was the minaret of the great mosque. Even today the city has an Eastern flavor, and anyone who climbs the ramps of the tower to the platform looks down on whitened courtyards between interlocked houses. He can see the large patio on the cathedral's north side, with its geometric irrigation ditches for the echeloned orange trees. The courtyard of the mosque is framed with arcades and entered through the "Gate of Pardon."

On July 8, 1401, the cathedral chapter determined to erect a church "so big and of such a type that whoever sees it completed will think we are mad." Unlike so many other ambitious projects, this plan became a reality.

The top of the Giralda is an artificial, almost phantasmagorical landscape: no roof covers the outer sides of vaults. Instead rounded "hills" bordered by masonried squares with the straight and almost horizontally articulated flying buttresses, together, form a bizarre, contradictory

---

The Giralda, the bell tower of the Seville cathedral, is actually the minaret of a mosque—heightened by a projection and crown—that once stood at this place.

110

A church implement almost unknown in Central Europe is the great Custodia, a tabernacle carried in feast processions. This elaborated, several-storied temple of silver belongs to Seville and was fashioned by Master Juan de Arfe.

whole. The main nave and transept are of different heights and each has its own windows.

Inside, however, as a heritage of the mosque, twilight, and a confusion of forms, prevail. One feels he is in an orderly grove of trees whose branches lose themselves in the climbing shadows. The disorientation is understandable. In most European churches choir and nave define front and rear. Here, however, the crossing is the exit point. The two central-nave bays contain the "Coro," with its choir stalls and two mighty organs with the typical horizontal "Spanish trumpets." The "Capilla Mayor," located east of the crossing and connected to the Coro by a narrow corridor, has two bays, as does the high altar.

Just as the cathedral itself holds the record for size among Spanish churches, the high altar at Seville is the largest in all Spain. Begun in 1482, and thus virtually the same age as the high altar at Chur, it follows completely different formal principles. Both are made of carved and gilded wood, but instead of a fixturelike shrine with movable leaves, Pieter Dancart, a Fleming, here chose the form of a wall that takes up the entire breadth of the nave and reaches to the very shoulders of the vaulting, where it is canopied by a projecting baldachin. Thirty-six compartments are joined in four ranks enclosed by filigreed Late Gothic tracery and by masterfully crafted pillars separated by figured tabernacles. The life of Christ is told in thirty-six scenes. Yet,

The tenebrous interior of the church—one of the largest in the world—expands in a hall style. It restricts the liturgical area at the crossing containing the high altar and choir stalls (on the left of the picture).

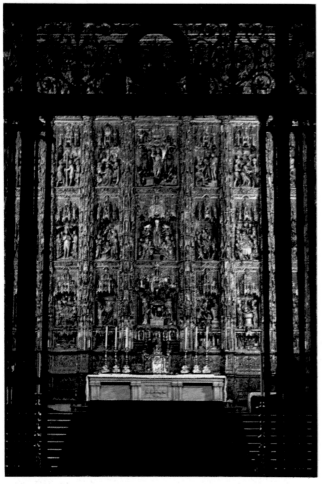

Surrounded by ornate grills, the gilded high altar in late Gothic style, sculpted from wood, covers the width of the central nave with a wall of pictures and rises up to the base of the vault arches. The Flemish artist Pieter Dancart began this incredible work in 1482.

standing in front of the altar, one can hardly concentrate on its theme. What prevails is an unreal golden glimmering in which detail vanishes.

Despite its dimensions—length: 446 feet (136 meters), continuous width: 233 feet (71 meters), summit of crossing: 184 feet (56 meters)—Seville cathedral conveys a peculiar restraint and austerity. The octagonal pillars surrounded by twenty-four shafts support simple crossribbed vaults. After the collapse of the original central tower in 1511 only the crossing and the nearby bays were furnished with intricate weblike ribs. The continuous midrib in the main nave shows the touch of a master who had contacts with England. Juan Norman is recorded as the builder of the first vault. Otherwise there is an almost complete lack of reliable information about the cathedral's construction. The five-nave plan may be the design of Alonso Martinez, who was named foreman in 1394. Maestro Carlin, probably Charles de Rouen, took over construction in 1439. Juan Norman was his successor, and finally, in 1496, a certain Ximon, possibly Simon of Burgos, became foreman.

At the end of the central nave lies the intimate Capilla Real, or Royal Chapel. It is built in the plateresque style, which superseded the Gothic in the sixteenth century and contains the baroque sarcophagus of the holy King Ferdinand. Here prayers are said before the patron saint of the city, Santa Maria de los Reyes. Candles and

More intimate structures adjoin the main cathedral, such as the plateresque Capilla Real on the east side. It contains the venerated picture of the city's patron saint, Santa Maria de los Reyes (background) and the sarcophagus of King Ferdinand (foreground).

hanging lamps spread a warm light and one is inclined to linger.

Westward past the forest of pillars and through a door in the north wall is the "Sagrario," or parish church, next to the cathedral. It is a well-proportioned, single-naved baroque room with side chapels, a space many bishops would gladly have as a principal church.

The sacristies, too, are virtual churches in themselves; they lead off from the south lateral nave and were built as rather grandiose monuments to Christopher Columbus, who embarked from the Seville harbor for his voyages of discovery. There are three sacristies: the Gothic-vaulted Vestry of the Chalice; the "Sacristia Mayor," a plateresque central room; and the chapter room, with an antique cupolaed dome in the form of an ellipse. All three are by the masters Diego di Riano and Martin Gainza and are textbook illustrations of Gothic forms evolving toward those of the Renaissance, as they did with the plateresque style in the sixteenth century. The word "plateresque" means "in the art of the silversmith," and indicates the

craftsman's reluctance to leave any surface unadorned.

The cathedral in Seville is one of the most richly endowed with works of art. As an example we choose not a Murillo or Velasquez but the great "custodia" of Master Juan de Arfe. This tabernacle, for transporting the consecrated Host in processions, is a miniature classical temple, as tall as a man, with a profusion of columns, entablatures, arches, balustrades, and figures. In Seville processions are a tradition; during Holy Week, the various congregations and brotherhoods with their devotional images move through the streets of the city, and the populace gives itself up entirely to this curiously festive lamentation, which reaches its height on Maundy Thursday and Good Friday. On these days the close connection between Spanish religion, art, and life are most apparent. Christ beneath the Cross, the agonized Virgin Mary, the scourged Jesus, are like members of the Spaniard's own family. He is familiar with them and suffers with them. Such rapport is practically unknown in the rest of Europe.

DURHAM

The Cathedral of Durham

Christianity came to Britain in 596 through the evangelical efforts of St. Augustine and his Benedictines. After the victory of William the Conqueror at Hastings in 1066, the English church was dominated by strong Norman personalities. This leadership was also reflected in the architecture of the great English cathedrals.

Bishop William of St. Carileph decided in 1093 to build a new mother church at Durham for his diocese, which had existed since 653. One of his motives for the project was to create a mighty bulwark against the Scots. The cathedral chapter at Durham was a Benedictine convent whose abbot was also bishop. Church and cloister lay serene and inaccessible on a hill above a bend in the Wear River. Many of the peculiarities of English cathedral construction which set it apart from continental designs are notable here: the great elongation with only modest vertical development; the preeminent position of the central tower over the crossing, which even subordinates the two towers of the west front when they exist at all; and the spaciousness of the choir, which is sometimes longer than the main nave.

One is at first tempted to "read" the layout of Durham in reverse. But here the front is not the great transept but the choir, which was placed on the site of the three original apses in the thirteenth century. The elegant chapel at the opposite end is not the so-called Lady Chapel, which in other English churches often terminates the choir. Rather it is a kind of porch, a "Galilee," which dates to 1175.

Norman architecture of the eleventh and twelfth centuries was extraordinarily advanced. The inner walls of the main church were divided not only into horizontal stories, in the style of the old Christian basilica, but also horizontally, with continuous vertical members rising toward the ceiling. At Durham the plan effectively utilizes the proportions of the square base of the transept (foreseen at St. Gall), and has the form of the piers alternate, according to whether they bisect the central-nave bays or simply separate the squared parts of the aisles. As a result the

117

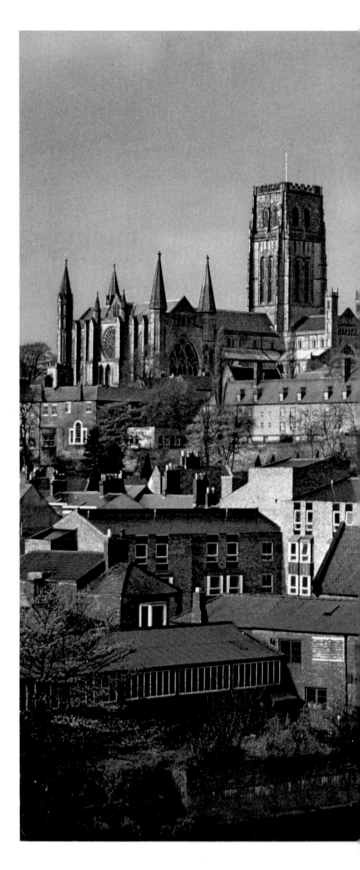

The cathedral and episcopal palace, each on its own hill, symbolize the spiritual and political power of the English bishops. The cathedral, begun in 1093, already shows the typical Anglo-Norman characteristics: extraordinary length, dominating central tower, and many subdivisions. At the east end can be seen the early Gothic transept with the Nine Altars.

The crossribbed vaults in the south aisle of the Durham choir are the earliest of their kind (after 1093).

side naves open into the bay corresponding with the central nave via two arches; Here too there are "strong" pillars and "weak" pillars. Even the ribbed vaults, so important in Gothic architecture, seem to have been used first in Norman construction. Those in the lateral nave south of the choir at Durham are among the oldest to survive.

When we compare Durham to Santiago de Compostela, built at the same time, the differences and similarities are clear. In both buildings one finds galleries above the side naves which open in double arches onto the central space. But Santiago is a triumph of order and regularity—the number of bays in the middle and lateral naves are equal, for example—while at Durham the difference between the strong and weak pillars is emphasized. Mighty round columns alternate with the clustered piers which divide the bays at the height of the lower floor and the galleries. At Santiago the main nave remains in darkness, for only the galleries and side naves are windowed. Durham, however, has its own clerestory, thanks to the advanced vaulting, so that the principal spaces are all equally illuminated. The galleries, in contrast to Santiago, are in twilight. In both structures the exterior is closed and fortresslike, almost without subdivision.

Inside one might expect to find a finely structured hall with rows of arches fading in the half-light. Instead modest piers offset their vast environs. The capitals are fashioned in the simplest shapes so as to unite the roundness of the supports with the rectangular abaci. Pronounced fluting in zigzag, waffle, or spiral patterns underlines the cylindrical wall modeling, but can scarcely be considered ornamentation. The sobriety of this interior will brook no adornment. Only in the western part of the cathedral

Considering the period when Durham was built, the use of varying or alternating
supports (for differentiated functions) is ahead of its time. Everybody who enters
this church is immediately impressed by the beauty and strength of the architecture.

and in the ground-floor arcades does one find the well-worn hallmark of Norman architecture, chevronlike denticulation.

The elemental beauty and strength of this architecture is so captivating that the visitor almost loses his eye for detail. He should notice the cross-shaped Gothic chapel of the "Nine Altars" (1235–1289). Another glory is the splendid "Neville Screen," a background facing for the high altar which separates the altar house from the Presbyterium. It features delicate pinnaclelike ornamentation, and in its tabernacles 107 alabaster statues once stood. The stone was transported by sea from France. Even the five-naved Romanesque Galilee, with its slender columns in clusters of four, cannot detract from the impact of the superbly integrated church space at Durham.

A look into the north transept makes the taut rigor of the architecture readily apparent. There are galleries above the arcades, and thanks to the use of crossribbed instead of barrel vaults, illumination of the upper recesses becomes possible. The great window in the front wall was introduced in the Gothic period.

LINCOLN

The Lincoln Cathedral

When construction began on the cathedral at Durham, Cluny was already under way. With its entrance hall, five naves, double transepts, and ambulatory with radiating chapels, it was to be the greatest Benedictine abbey church in the West. The influence of Cluny is apparent in many parts of Europe and is strongly reflected in the English church, founded by monks and monastic in character. On the other hand, England did not borrow all the Clunian incidentals. The ambulatory, for example, remained alien to Britain. But again and again we encounter the double transept, so that the typical British cathedral plan looks like a patriarchal cross with two bars.

Lincoln Cathedral belongs to this tradition, although it was not a conventual church but was staffed by secular priests. Not as assertive as its sister at Durham, it majestically crowns a knoll with its three slim towers, the largest of which, over the crossing, once had a wooden steeple reputedly 525 feet (160 meters) high. The city nestles close on the west; the other sides are surrounded by green, as are the cloister and

chapter house. The latter, a decagonal building, is positioned like a grand sculpture on the lawn. Its builder used unique free-standing buttresses against the thrust of the vaulting; inside a central pillar gathers in the ribs arching from the corners. These counterforts look like royal bodyguards stationed at a discreet distance from their king. Elegantly fashioned arches also absorb stress.

Lincoln was originally a Norman church, of which the west front and tower substructures survive. The rest was destroyed by an earthquake on April 15, 1185. A year later one Hugo, a Carthusian from Avalon, was consecrated Bishop of Lincoln. In 1192 he commissioned Master Geoffrey de Noiers for a new building, which began, as was generally the case in the Middle Ages, with the choir. Geoffrey adopted the new architectural formalism of France. But despite his Gallic name, he had grown up in Britain and his work was to bear a distinctively English stamp. English High Gothic did not follow the strict systematization and verticality of the contemporary French

An integral feature of the English cathedral is the chapter house, usually an independent structure used for meetings of the cathedral chapter. At Lincoln the early Gothic house features free-standing piers appended to the building with flying buttresses.

After the destructive earthquake of 1185, Geoffrey de Noiers began reconstruction of the cathedral in the new Gothic form from France. Like many of its sisters, Lincoln borrows the concept of the double transept from the abbey church of Cluny. The central tower once had a wooden steeple that apparently reached a height of 525 feet (160 meters).

cathedrals. It preferred rather a free, "additive" composition, moderated and accommodating, with many independent elements. In Britain the vertical articulation of Late Gothic became compatible with the horizontal.

The piers of the main nave, with their almost perfectly round shafts, are the sole support of the arcades. The triforium—a dark area beneath the side-nave walls, not the narrow passageway of French cathedrals—rushes in a horizontal row of arches to the choir. The generous profile of the arch does not echo the form of the shafts but is much more picturesque. The English predilection for the picturesque effect also accounts for the frequent use of dark Purbeck marble next to the lighter brick masonry. Closings and screens divide the sanctuary into nave, choir, presbytery, and so-called retrochoir.

The choir and transept attest to Master Geoffrey's original mind and his pleasure in the unusual and surprising. Among his pioneering innovations is the rib at the top of the vaulting, which was to become an earmark of English vaulting. Geoffrey could not have known that his unique vaulting over the choir—he replaced usual crossribbing with a four-rayed fan— would find successors in the Late Gothic. The new vaulting was considered grotesque by his peers, and the less-gifted master who completed the nave reverted to the midrib. Geoffrey also created two blind arcades, one behind the other, and designed the transept vertically to afford surprising perspectives.

Today, the Angel Choir (1256–1320) has replaced the original choir area. It is regarded as the most richly decorated Gothic church room in England, and illustrates why the English call their form of High Gothic the "decorated style." Blossoms burst not only on the capitals but from between the columns of the triforium, from the pillars, out of the necks of the arches, and among the traceries. Bright stone alternates with dark. In the arch spandrels of the triforium music-making and incense-laden angels disport around figures of Mary and the Christ Child. The tracery at the eastern closing is a single glass wall with eight lancets gathered repeatedly into arches. The entire window materializes out of one motif.

Thus the art of the British Isles, at first glance so eccentric, has a distinct role in the development of medieval church architecture. It finds its place in the timeless metaphor implied by all religious art, which provides a way for mortal eyes to view the eternal.

Today we are spiritually more remote from the baroque than the baroque was from the High Middle Ages. Perhaps it is good to consider the works of earlier epochs. They are grand achievements that say more to us, perhaps, than the written word. This book will have served its true purpose if it inspires the reader to visit these cathedrals and perhaps to receive there a measure of the harmony they embody.

The Angel Choir, with its myriad decorations, its contrasting of light and dark stone, its sculptures and tracery, is the richest Gothic church space in England. The continuous longitudinal rib is characteristically English.

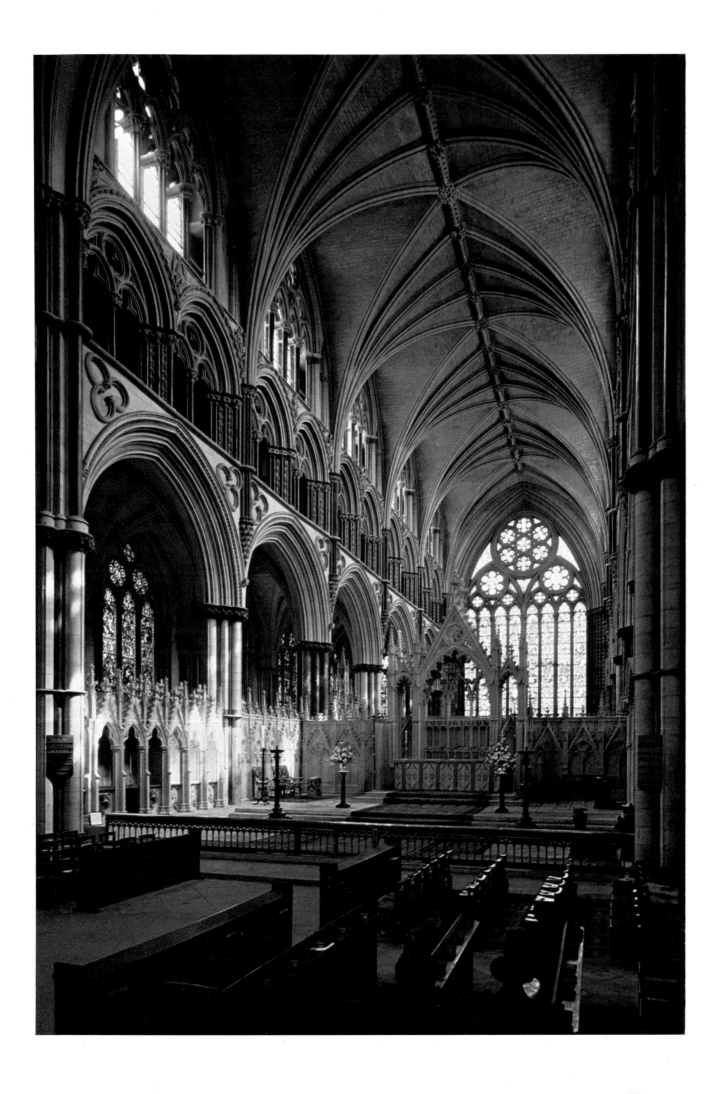